What people are say

Georgian Port

What happens after a revolution, when the bright and shiny finish has worn off its ideals? In this book, the fragmented and often paradoxical changes wrought by Georgia's Rose Revolution appear in the form of killer mermaids, Stalin statues, Potemkin villages painted in candy colors and other surreal objects. Capturing the weirdness and the wonder of post-revolutionary Georgia, Frederiksen and Gotfredsen also capture people's very real struggles to get by, their fears of war and their dreams of a "European" future. Beautifully and hauntingly written, this book captures not only Georgia's politics, but its soul.
Elizabeth Cullen Dunn, author of *Privatizing Poland: Baby Food, Big Business and the Remaking of Labor*

Revolutions are as much made of dreams as real events, and these dreams have afterlives as ghosts as the revolutionary hope fades into disappointment or despair. Writing the history of a revolutionary period is difficult, especially writing one that deals with the fundamentally emergent nature of a revolutionary period, as this one does, embracing the confusion of tenses in which the present is pregnant with the future and the future becomes a past as a condition of narration. This book tracks the lively history of Rose Revolutionary Georgia in a lovely and vivid manner, an engaging narrative full of lively characters, beginning always from small things and local perspectives that show the Rose Revolutionary period as a series of hopes and dreams, programs and disappointments. Misha Saakashvili appears throughout, sometimes as a real historical person, sometimes also an imagined demiurge, sometimes a fraudulent trickster. The ways a revolution changes a society are here portrayed from

many perspectives, and the way the revolutionary dreams sometimes became haunting ghosts shows how a single moment can become a whole period of social life.
Paul Manning, author of *Love Stories: Private Love and Public Romance in Georgia*

This book is crafted as a compendium of tacit knowledge about Georgia, harboring an array of insights that capture the tensions and ambiguities of a country that finds itself back from the future and poised between assembly and disassembly. The image of the portrait is therefore very accurate, reflecting the make-believe realities and re-enactments faced by the authors. Thumbing through its pages, I discovered how anthropological variations can be interwoven through biographies, social affects and political afterlives. This type of scholarship is not only inspiring and informative, but also pleasure to read.

Georgia is a country for storytellers and vernacular Sisyphus of life, Martin Demant Frederiksen and Katrine Bendtsen Gotfredsen being the perfect examples of this contagious ardor. The intimate and sharp look achieved by the authors makes this collection an important milestone in the discussion of contemporary social dynamics in Eastern Europe and the understanding of the human condition overall.
Francisco Martínez, author of *Playgrounds and Battlefields: Critical Perspectives of Social Engagement*

Georgian Portraits

Essays on the Afterlives of a Revolution

Georgian Portraits

Essays on the Afterlives of a Revolution

Martin Demant Frederiksen

& Katrine Bendtsen Gotfredsen

zero books

Winchester, UK
Washington, USA

First published by Zero Books, 2017
Zero Books is an imprint of John Hunt Publishing Ltd., Laurel House, Station Approach,
Alresford, Hants, SO24 9JH, UK
office1@jhpbooks.net
www.johnhuntpublishing.com
www.zero-books.net

For distributor details and how to order please visit the 'Ordering' section on our website.

ISBN: 978 1 78535 362 8
978 1 78535 363 5 (ebook)
Library of Congress Control Number: 2016951895

A CIP catalogue record for this book is available from the British Library.

Design: Stuart Davies

Printed and bound by CPI Group (UK) Ltd, Croydon, CR0 4YY, UK

CONTENTS

Also by the authors

Martin Demant Frederiksen:

Young Men, Time, and Boredom in the Republic of Georgia. Philadelphia: Temple University Press, 2013

Ethnographies of Youth and Temporality – Time Objectified. Philadelphia: Temple University Press, 2014 (co-edited with Anne Line Dalsgaard, Lotte Meinert and Susanne Højlund)

Ethnographies of Grey Zones in Eastern Europe – Borders, Relations and Invisibilities. London: Anthem Press, 2015 (co-edited with Ida Harboe Knudsen)

Katrine Bendtsen Gotfredsen:

Evasive Politics: Paradoxes of History, Nation and Everyday Communication in the Republic of Georgia. PhD Dissertation, Department of Anthropology, University of Copenhagen, 2013

We would like to dedicate this book to coincidence, which, from 2004 up until publication, has been a guiding principle. That, and Ann Louise Slot (who will know why).

Preface

In some ways, this all started during a month spent in desolate locations in Poland in January 2003, where we decided that we would at some point soon travel together to some place further south. Through a series of random events and decisions we ended up buying tickets that would bring us from Russia over Armenia to Georgia the following year. This journey became decisive in many aspects of our lives, among those being the hours, days and years of discussions that eventually came to form the basis of the coming pages.

Throughout the years following our first stay in Georgia, a number of institutions have financially supported the various trips and research projects upon which this book is based, including the Danish Council for Independent Research; The Ethnographic Collections at Moesgaard Museum; The Klaus Ferdinand Memorial Fund; The Department of Anthropology, University of Copenhagen; and the Oticon Foundation. Although the respective grants we received were aimed at different goals than this book, we would not have been able to write it without their generous support.

Elizabeth Cullen Dunn and Maria Louw were kind enough to comment on a very early draft of the first chapters. The outline of the book was presented at Free University of Tbilisi as part of the Free University Research Seminars. We would like to thank all the participants of this event for their comments and suggestions, and especially Tamta Khalvashi for arranging it. We would also like to thank Renee Čaleta Meroni, who hosted us in her wonderful house during a writing retreat in Croatia in the spring of 2016, and provided us with the perfect context for thinking through our material.

And finally, we owe our sincere gratitude to the wonderful people in Georgia who have shared their time, their friendship and their stories with us during the preceding 12 years. One of the goals of this book has been to put forth stories that would otherwise have gone untold, and it goes without saying that any responsibility for the contents of what follows is ours alone.

– MDF and KBG, Croatia (and other places) 2016

Introduction

An Event

It started on a November evening in 2003 in a small country that few in the Western world knew much of. A man walked the streets with a mission. He was joined by thousands of people and, although he was not as such their leader, he told them to hold hands while they surrounded a building in a central part of the nation's capital. After this he told them to disperse, which they did. They all met again in the following days, and, in the end, he and others in the group entered the building exclaiming "Resign, resign!" The building that was entered housed the parliament of the Republic of Georgia and the person he addressed was the president in office, Eduard Shevardnadze. The man himself was the young lawyer Mikheil Saakashvili, member of a coalition seeking to overthrow Shevardnadze by peaceful means. The event that was taking place would later be named the Revolution of Roses. According to one version the name was given because protesters had handed out roses to the soldiers assigned to stop them. In another account it was because Saakashvili held a rose in his hand as he entered the parliament building.

Saakashvili was by no means alone in arranging what took place, but he became the spearhead and symbol of the revolution and its promises. For the same reasons, he would also become the symbol of its later failures. At the time of the revolution Saakashvili was looked upon as a hero, particularly among the younger segments of society. Some referred to him as "crazy Misha" due to his at times frantic style, but nevertheless – or perhaps exactly because of this – many saw him as an epithet of a strong, Georgian man; good-hearted and emotional.[1] Being good-hearted and good-souled (*kai guli da kai suli* in Georgian) is an honoured trademark of masculinity in the country – a sign of both strength and bravery as well as a sign of the well-spirited provider of family and host of guests. Saakashvili was a fighter, but most importantly, he was a Georgian.

The period immediately before and after the revolution was one of excitement. Travelling through the region at the time, we were met by an atmosphere of optimism and hopeful sentiments. This was not merely so in the capital where the revolution itself had taken place. In the small city Akhaltsikhe, near the border to Turkey, young people would walk the streets in the evening carrying EU flags as signals of Georgia having taken the first step towards being a democratic, European country. As there was no electricity, the streets they walked in were pitch-dark so the flags were barely visible, but the joyful voices emerging from the darkness seemed confident that soon, very soon, both electricity and the EU would be part of daily life.

The revolution had been peaceful in the sense that no armed forces had used physical power. But despite this, and despite the optimistic sentiments emerging throughout the country, it was not a period without tension. This was not least the case in the Adjara region in western Georgia. Along with two other regions, South Ossetia and Abkhazia, Adjara was an autonomous republic – a status given in Soviet times. A few months after Saakashvili was officially voted president, the leader of Adjara, Aslan Abashidze, was ousted and the region came under the full control of the government in Tbilisi. Adjara would be heralded as the first major success of the new government and taken as a sign that in the two other regions the same would soon occur.

On a general level, there were few who had any exact idea about what would happen after the revolution. Only that something would, and already was. In that sense it was not merely a situation of optimism and hope, it was also one of confusion and uncertainty. And as years passed by, it would be the latter rather than the former taking precedence amassing to experiences of scepticism and disillusion, and even paranoia and conspiracy.

Much has been written about the geopolitical significance of this event; about the possible foreign involvement in the revolution itself; about the ways in which it altered Georgia's relations to neighbouring Russia; about its significance as a precursor to the revolutions in Ukraine and Kyrgyzstan. But exactly what happened to the revolution after it ended? How may we understand its aftermaths and possible continuing significance? In this book we chronicle aspects of everyday life in the Republic of Georgia since the Rose Revolution in 2003 up until the present, and we explore how the visions supporting the revolution seeped into the everyday life of ordinary Georgians. What can we learn, we ask, not just about the Republic of Georgia at present, but also about post-revolutionary settings at large, by looking at the social afterlives of the Rose Revolution?

Afterlives and the end of new beginnings

With this book we wish to make two contributions. Firstly, we seek to present insights into contemporary Georgia. In this respect the book can be read as a solely empirical piece providing depictions of places, people and themes that have marked both politics and everyday realities within the last decade, as well as descriptions of key cultural self-representations that are employed both on political and everyday social levels. Secondly, we wish to shed light on post-revolutionary settings on a more general level. We do so not by comparing our material to other revolutionary situations, but by providing a framework through which political events and aftermaths in similar contexts may be approached. In the following paragraphs we will elaborate on the latter.

In its popular usage, "afterlife" denotes a realm in which the consciousness of an individual continues to reside after the death of the body. Recent theoretical developments within anthropology and related disciplines have argued for the use of "afterlives" as an analytical notion through which to understand processes of socio-political change. In her work on imperial debris, Laura Ann Stoler for instance has argued that in order to understand the life of people who live in situations marked by disintegration, we need to focus on the social and material afterlives of structures, sensibilities and things.[2] That is, we must focus on that which continues to linger in an altered form. As several studies of socio-political change in the former Soviet republics have shown, the new beginning presented by the end of the Soviet era did not entail that a new and better future was waiting accessibly around the corner. Indeed, in Georgia it was partly the widespread disillusionment over the lack of change achieved by President Eduard Shevardnadze that led to the revolution. Similarly, beyond the political-institutional sphere, "revolutions" can only be a metaphor masking inevitable continuities of social organization and everyday practices.[3] In that sense, the Rose Revolution did not entail a radical or all-encompassing form of socio-political change taking place overnight. Indeed, as critical observers of the politics conducted following the revolution noted: the roses had thorns. Our intention in what follows, however, is not to evaluate the success-rate of the revolution in terms of indicators of democratization, good governance or economic development. Rather, we approach it as an event that – for better and worse – had social consequences and effects beyond its own political visions and outside explicitly political domains. Just as the lingering remnants of the Soviet period have been explored in several studies of the post-Soviet region, our intention here is to explore what has lingered in the wake and aftermath of the revolution.

Using social afterlives as a vantage point allows us to confront the apparent contradiction that although political periods and events may be over, they continue to live on as memories and practices, at times even as haunting presences or forms of nostalgia for that which never came to be.[4] Moreover, as will become apparent, visions and afterlives created by revolutionary situations are not only uncontrollable but also work back on the political. In that sense, our aim is to present an understanding of politics and political change not by looking at politics itself, but by exploring that which goes on around it, and to depict the effects and affects of political change on a micro-level. Said differently, we do not have our primary focus on classical themes regarding politics and political change such as reforms processes, the workings of state-institutions, or international relations. This is not to render such themes irrelevant but rather to present a supplementary perspective on the contemporary Georgian socio-political reality. In taking this approach we are writing from a post-Marxist perspective, following the likes of Cornelius Castoriadis and Vladimir Tismaneanu in seeing the similarities of political systems such as communism and capitalism or neoliberalism rather than focusing on essentialist oppositions.[5] These perspectives are unfolded in the conclusion in relation to the empirical cases that are presented throughout the book.

Portraits and Variations

Milan Kundera writes of *The Book of Laughter and Forgetting* that it is a novel in the form of variations: "the various parts follow each other like the various stages of a voyage leading into the interior of a thought, the interior of a single, unique situation, the understanding of which recedes from my sight into the distance".[6] Methodologically we take a similar approach in this book. The variations that follow take the shape of portraits, the interior they lead to being the unique situation of the Rose Revolution. The portraits – or variations – that are presented, however, do not lead toward the revolution but rather depart from it. They describe, each in their own way, the revolution as it took form in the ten-year period following November 2003, and how it ceased to be an event but became part of social life. The portraits are sequenced chronologically and although they concern different places, people, events or things, they generate each other's context. That is, they extend each other as case studies of smaller events that are all somehow related to a larger one – the revolution. Taken together, we term these portraits "afterlives" of the revolution in order to convey how the political ideas and visions underpinning the revolution took on new, sometimes surprising or unintended, lives of their own as they met social reality.

During the ten-year period depicted, we have both spent a couple of years of our lives conducting anthropological research in Georgia, spread over various times and places, with different aims and among different people. We first visited the country a few months after the revolution occurred, and to a large extent it has been through the revolution and its aftermaths that we came to know the country. This book is an attempt to share that knowledge. As previously mentioned, the following chapters may be read solely as empirical descriptions of various aspects of everyday social life in Georgia over the past ten years. Behind each portrait, however, more general analytical themes linger; themes that in various ways resonate with recent studies of the post-Soviet region, as well as studies of socio-political change and revolutionary situations on a broader level. These include questions of self-representation, disillusion, displacement, iconoclasm, performativity, scepticism, conspiracy and phantasm, to mention a few.

The fall of the Soviet Union necessitated the construction of new political identities across the region. Novel political projects and appeals for support were often framed as (highly emotional) "national", "traditional" or "cultural" awakenings promising a prosperous future through the return to pre-Soviet identities.[7] Several of the coming chapters engage these frameworks. Most of the people and figures we are to meet spend much representational work and energy in defining, categorizing and comprehending national, traditional, religious and other group identities. Analytically such processes have fostered a particular attention to the symbols and acts involved in "socializing" landscapes and imbuing places with (new) political values; for instance in the form of iconoclasm[8] – the tearing down and erection of monuments,[9] buildings, and even entire neighbourhoods.[10] Even so, as we shall come to show, former social practices, visions and subjectivities keep lingering behind novel ones as "ruins",[11] "post-presences"[12] or even as haunting ghosts.[13] The Rose Revolution and its aftermath may be seen as a "second wave" of such iconoclasm, symbolically and practically breaking not only with the Soviet past but also the first decade of independence.

Another set of studies of the post-Soviet context also resonating with the upcoming chapters have focused on questions of dispossession and disillusionment,[14] post-socialist nostalgia[15] and changing and emerging forms of (inter)subjectivity, personhood and social being.[16] Oftentimes, such studies have entailed a focus on changing perceptions of time and the role of hope and magic in societies marked by uncertainty and change,[17] paralleled by another set of themes such as paranoia, suspicion and conspiracy, seen as (re)actions, or even symptoms, of an obsession with transparency in what appears to be an opaque and inaccessible social world of influences and powers.[18] What all these diverse approaches engage, then, are the everyday responses to uncertainty, ambiguity and changes in the social fabric caused by overarching political change.

Relating to all these diverse, yet interconnected, themes are more overarching questions of political form, practice and performance.[19] That is, how political order as well as change is symbolized and performed, and the now and then paradoxical effects and practices underpinning such explicit articulations. Each of the chapters in the book will, through an individual concluding coda, engage with one or several of the above themes.

The codas provide analytical meta-readings of the individual portraits, but these sections of the book may also be seen as an introduction to central themes and debates within anthropological studies of the post-Soviet region.

In the chapters that follow, we depart from Tbilisi, the physical centre of the event, and move on to other places, particularly the cities of Gori and Batumi. We return to Tbilisi now and then, with stops on the way. This in some sense renders this a travel account, but not in a geographical sense. Rather, it is a journey through a theme, a movement through a short but significant part of Georgia's recent history; one that will inevitably live on as a trace, as an afterlife, both materially, socially and symbolically. We write about the *afterlives* of the revolution because it is likely to remain an unfinished story; the political figures and institutions underlying it may have been replaced with something different, but something of it will inevitably live on, just as the more distant pasts lived on through the period we describe. This, then, could perhaps best be described as a peculiar form of an obituary of something gone but not lost or over.

Form and escalation

In a country of myth, it is little wonder that we in the upcoming pages will meet a mermaid, a soldier, a winemaker, a shade of colour, a make-believe invasion and a real one, people who do not officially exist, a dreamer, an unbuilt city, a theatre of politics and a mother figure. These are not fictional characters however. The chapters in the book each describe a figure embodying a particular aspect of Georgia and the decade following the revolution. While they are all connected to an aspect of the revolution and its afterlives they also engage more general – now and then stereotypical – aspects of Georgian history, nationality, socio-cultural ideals and everyday social life. The chapters will progress chronologically in a triple sense: they move from the early days immediately after the revolution towards the eventual fall of Saakashvili's government. The contextual information surrounding the figures we describe moves from the distant past towards increasingly utopian and distant futures. And the sentiments described and conveyed move from optimism through scepticism and ambivalence towards what seems like farce and absurdity. It is with this structure that we seek to convey the way in which some of the visions of the revolution have escalated beyond their own foundational principles.[20] That is, to repeat, how the afterlives of the revolution can be traced in different aspects of social reality.

In Chapters 1 and 2 we meet two archetypes of Georgian social and cultural life: the winemaker and the mother. These chapters act as backgrounds for understanding the basis of Georgian socio-cultural ideals and daily life in independent Georgia. However, besides providing a background to Georgia and the revolution, they also illustrate the tension between on the one hand ideals and explicit cultural representations and on the other hand lived everyday life, by presenting two radically different perspectives and experiences of the same political event. Chapter 1, "The Winemaker", portrays Beka. He is a man embodying (and adhering to) many local, cultural traditions, such as making wine, being head of a family and entertaining guests. Through the story of Beka and his vivid representations of Georgian nationality and tradition, we recount in this chapter central elements of Georgia's cultural history, the hopeful sentiments surrounding the time of the revolution and the interrelation of the two. The second chapter, "The Mother", portrays Marina, a woman living in the old town of Tbilisi with her mother and daughter. Through Marina's story we depict the image of the mother in Georgia as well as the differences existing between generations – from nostalgia towards the Soviet past to hopes for the future. Marina's story furthermore illustrates a perceived lack of immediate change after revolution and the dire situation that was continuously faced by many citizens in the country.

Chapters 3 to 5 each in their way describe concrete social effects created by the new political visions, policies and practices that saw the light of day in the first years following the revolution. By describing living people who officially ceased to exist, façade colours and surface restorations masking dilapidated buildings, and war and national patriotism mixed with ambivalence, this group of chapters engage with the oftentimes contradictory and paradoxical relationship between what we may term "form" and "content" of the post-revolutionary visions and practices. Chapter 3, "The Misfits", portrays a series of people in central Tbilisi who in each their way were misfits in relation to the vision and rhetoric of the revolution: beggars, street children, internally displaced people (IDPs) and a street musician. Politically they were seen as symbolic images of the turmoil and social problems of the 1990s, and their presence thus went against the political rhetoric claiming that the so-called post-Soviet transition had come to an end. Chapter 4, "The Pastel Shade", portrays the painting of facades in a series of major cities in the country. First undertaken prior to a visit from then-US president George W. Bush, and hence signifying a new political allegiance with the West, the painting of facades became some of the first material signs of change. However, they also became some of the first sources of critique. Chapter 5, "The Soldier", portrays the Georgian-Russian war in August 2008. More specifically it examines the image of the soldier as it has been put forth as a symbol of Georgian patriotism and military progress after the revolution. This symbolic figure of the soldier is contrasted and compared to a persistent image from the country's Soviet past that still – even after the revolution and the 2008 war – enjoys popular appeal: that of Joseph Stalin as a Georgian national playing a vital role in the outcome of WWII.

Chapters 6 to 9 describe what seems to be an escalating atmosphere of rumour and paranoia accompanied by disillusion, and an increased decoupling of visions and political performance from practice and experience. Chapter 6, "The Mermaid", portrays the rumoured discovery of a mermaid in a small village on the Black Sea coast. While many of the elderly and middle-aged citizens in the area looked upon this discovery with anxiety, it was regarded by youths with ridicule. Through the story of the mermaid, the chapter depicts the scepticism and disillusion among the generation of youths who came of age during the time of the revolution; their loss of belief not only in religion or magic, but also in the state itself. Chapter 7, "The Hoax", portrays a news segment aired on the local TV station Imedi claiming a new Russian invasion to be in progress. The immediate popular reactions – panic and uproar – pointed to a general atmosphere of paranoia and conspiracy that has been produced and nurtured through ideas of persistent dangers to the Georgian nation and, in effect, the revolutionary cause. Chapter 8, "The Theatre" portrays local perceptions of politics as a performance. It revolves around the project of building hospitals in all middle-sized cities of Georgia and the locally known fact that they were built mainly to be opened and left without contents (neither material nor staff). Returning to perspectives from formerly introduced persons, such as Marina, this chapter depicts how politics increasingly comes to be seen as a theatre or spectacle. Chapter 9 portrays a city not yet built. Lazika, "The Emerald City", was a project devised by the government with the aim of building a power centre for economic trade in the Black Sea region. The planned location was close to the border of Abkhazia – one of the two autonomous regions within Georgia recognized by Russia as independent. Although financially supported by neoliberal forces such as Donald Trump, Lazika was widely criticized locally as a return to neo-bolshevism not least due to the planned relocation of existing villages in the area.

The final portrait, Chapter 10, is of the politician and businessman Bidzina Ivanishvili who led the "Georgian Dream" coalition that won the 2012 parliamentary elections and effectively ended the unilateral reign of Saakashvili and his United National Movement. Up until then a largely reclusive figure, Ivanishvili is held by many to have gained popularity not because of his political vision but rather because of him not being Saakashvili. In this final portrait, we depict him as a character, and examine how he as a figure both resembles and deviates from that of Saakashvili, and we explore the local perception of him as an embodiment of the end of the Rose Revolution. From initially being a figure embodying strength, progress and democratic change, it would ironically be Saakashvili's admittance of defeat to Ivanishvili that came to be seen as one of his greatest democratic achievements.

Returning to the notion of afterlives, the Conclusion includes a series of considerations concerning the legacies of the revolution and the possible recycling of political practices in years to come. In doing so, we will discuss which traces of the revolution there are to be seen in current social and political developments. Studies of the post-Soviet region have within recent years been criticized of failing to engage an audience beyond its own circle. In the conclusion we will draw on the codas of each chapter and engage in a broader discussion about how debates and insights from the field of post-Soviet studies may be used in more general understandings of revolutionary changes and their aftermaths beyond both Georgia and the post-Soviet context – including, among other things, how the outcome of social or revolutionary change may best be seen as a form of spiralling, despite being politically premised on notions of linearity.

Before we set off, it should be noted that many of the voices and perspectives we will encounter in the following chapters are critical. This should not be read as a sign of Saakashvili and his government not having any supporters in the years after the revolution. On the contrary, many Georgians remained loyal to the president and his political visions throughout his time in power. However, as we are interested in the unintended as much as the intended outcomes of the revolution, the ten portraits presented are ones that seek to go behind, or below, official representations and visions.

Chapter 1

The Winemaker

Arrival

We are forced to exit the bus and walk into Georgia as we reach the border. This is to the obvious discontent of the other passengers as we are already hours late. The ride from Yerevan in Armenia has been painstakingly slow due to the dire condition of the vehicle – an old Soviet school bus. An armed soldier escorts us to a small shed that makes up the Armenian-Georgian border post at Sadakhlo, a deserted landscape in what seems to be the middle of nowhere. Once seated inside the shed, an officer looks through our passports and examines the visa we obtained through the Georgian Consulate in Yerevan. We have no shared language to communicate in and he looks at us with a significant amount of scepticism, as if thinking: "Why on earth are you coming here?"

The exact reasons as to why we had gone in the first place are blurry: a shared fascination with the post-Soviet region; a shared non-existent knowledge of the Caucasus region which resided on the map as a question mark; a shared bottle of red wine (perhaps several) and a decision to buy tickets and go. Both anthropology students at the time, little did we know that this three-week stay in Georgia would come to define our later academic lives.

Entering the country at this time, July 2004, was a slightly arduous affair. With our national backgrounds we needed a formal invitation from a local institution in order to get the necessary stamps for visits longer than two weeks. We obtained it by searching for local NGOs on the Internet, writing as many as we could to ask them to help us. Nina, an office manager who worked in one of these, replied. Not only did she assist us in how to obtain our visas, she also offered us to stay with her and her family in their newly built farmhouse and hotel outside Tbilisi.

We had initially wanted to visit all three countries in the Southern Caucasus – Armenia, Georgia and Azerbaijan, and if possible also parts of the Russian side of the mountains further north. But many borders in the region could not be crossed due to political conflicts. Borders and visa procedures thus framed our itinerary. We could obtain a visa for Georgia at a consulate in Armenia's capital Yerevan, and we could obtain a visa for Armenia online.

After a few weeks in Armenia we embark on the old school bus-cum-long-distance bus, with our visas in hand. The sceptical officer at the Sadakhlo border crossing eventually warms to us as we discover a shared interest in our cigarettes, and after a good while we re-enter the bus with stamps in our passports and drive on towards Tbilisi. The bus fights bravely on the last hilly stretches of road, coughing and shaking. We arrive in a suburb, on a street that has no visible signs of being a bus station. All we have is Nina's phone number but upon calling her we have no idea as to how we can explain to her where we are. Signposts and street names are written in an intricate alphabet we are not yet familiar with and the only landmarks on the street are a series of small newspaper and cigarette vendors. The sun is setting and the sound of generators increases in volume. Throughout the 1990s – and at this point still – electricity shortages were a recurrent part of everyday life.[1] Blending into this is the frequent sound of car alarms going off, all yelling the same tune from inside rampant vehicles. We hand the cell phone to a young man standing nearby who explains to Nina where we are. Having received it back, Nina tells us to stay where we are and that her husband, Beka, will pick us up as soon as he can.

For some odd reason we are not in doubt that it is Beka arriving when a large Land Rover approaches us at high speed. He gets out of the car with a convivial smile on his face bursting into a heavy laugh as we explain our journey on the bus. He is a sturdy, not-so-tall figure with short black hair and lively eyes. Although his car suggests that he is likely to be better off financially than many others, his strong hands reveal that he is not unaccustomed to manual labour. Our backpacks are thrown into the car and we are seated in the back. Beka, as we learn immediately, is not concerned with speed limits. Despite his rapid driving however he is fully able to describe the parts of the city we move through. In particular, he highlights the Old Town with its labyrinth-like small streets crammed with traditional, wooden houses and balconies. Many of the houses are rundown and stand as testimonies to the economic stagnation that has marked the country since 1991. He points out old houses of worship, home to a variety of different religions. Some stand almost side by side; a Synagogue, an Armenian Apostolic Church, a Russian Orthodox Church, a Georgian Orthodox Church, and not far from there a Mosque. Tbilisi was a multicultural city in ancient times, he tells us, a junction on the Silk Road and home to a myriad of different nationalities and ethnicities.[2] This spot of the Old Town, he explains, is an illustrative example of Georgian tolerance and co-habitation with other ethnic groups and religious communities over the centuries.

Moving further through the city we pass the parliament building on Rustaveli Avenue. "During the Tbilisi War back in the early nineties", Beka recounts, "fighting factions took their place on each side of this avenue and one could not pass for gunshots crossing the street". Neighbours, classmates and even family members would fight each other. The civil war had erupted between supporters of the country's first president, Zviad Gamsakhurdia, and his opponents shortly after Georgia gained independence. It was a fight for power and for the right to define what the nation was and where its boundaries should be drawn. Beka does not elaborate on the degree of his own involvement nor which side of the avenue he had been on.

At the end of the avenue Hotel Iveria towers on the right side of the street. Originally built in the 1960s as a luxury hotel it now houses refugees from the war in Abkhazia. Conflicts in Abkhazia and South Ossetia had escalated alongside the civil war in Georgia proper. The two territories, formerly the South Ossetian Autonomous Oblast and the Autonomous Republic of Abkhazia, declared independence from Georgia in the early 1990s following the dissolution of the Soviet Union, and over a quarter of a million ethnic Georgians were forced to leave the Abkhazia and South Ossetia at this time. Having their own specific trajectories, the two territories have both been centres of conflict and dispute since then, and even if they are *de jure* considered part of the Georgian republic, they are to this day *de facto* independent, with support from Russia. Bringing them back under Georgian control, however, is one of the main declared missions of the new president.

Although the situation somewhat stabilized in the mid-nineties, when the former Communist leader Eduard Shevardnadze had become the country's second president, the nineties altogether were times of organized crime, lawlessness, fighting and shortage of everything from bread and potatoes to gas and electricity. Under Shevardnadze's leadership Georgia gained a reputation as one of the most corrupt countries in the world. Now, Beka notes to us, luckily, things are becoming different. The replacement of Shevardnadze with the young reformer Mikheil Saakashvili in the presidential office promises new times ahead not just in terms of corruption but also in terms of territorial integrity.

The winemaker

We leave Tbilisi and ascend one of the surrounding hillsides. For now, we also leave behind discussions of politics. Beka moves with great ease along the winding road and makes frequent use of his horn to alert other drivers that he has no intention of slowing down or changing whatever lane he is driving in, or to let them know that he intends to overtake on the inside. We are driving towards Kiketi, a small area in the woods mainly consisting of *dachas* – summer houses. There are no street names in these parts of the woods, Beka laughingly tells us as we enter a steep gravel road. At the end of the road we stop before a giant metal gate behind which Beka's dacha is located. He inherited the lot from his grandfather and a new house was built there recently. Beka is an architect by education and he has designed the new four-story farmhouse himself. Besides Nina and Beka, the household consists of their two young sons, Nina's mother, and their Russian nanny. They greet us as we exit the car and we are led inside.

Asides from being an architect, Beka is a businessman, but more importantly, he is a winemaker. When we first met him he was in an early stage of experimentation, making only wine for himself and his family. He was not alone in his great love of wine, Georgia being one of the world's oldest wine-producing nations, as he is quick to inform us. He experiments with both red and white wines, as well as the local spirit *chacha*. His initial experiments have focused on making both wine and chacha strong. And they are. His friends and family members joke about their fear of Beka showing up with large quantities of homemade wine which would leave them with no choice but to drink it with him and face the headaches that would follow. This mockery notwithstanding, Beka is a well-liked and much-respected man by those who know him. Everyone we meet praises him as an honourable, strong, poetic, emotional, hospitable and kind man. An archetypical Georgian, we are told.

Beka's primary agenda as our host in the following weeks is to thoroughly introduce us to the Georgian *supra* in which his wine is a central element. The supra, literally "tablecloth", is a ritualized feast with elaborate toasting and drinking. The toasts are proposed by the appointed head of the table, the *tamada*, and occasionally, if allowed, elaborated on by the other participants.

The toasts of the supra include the wider issues and emotions of life and living, and the toasts to particular people and events hence become a means of engaging and representing ideals pertaining to national traditions, family values, God, life, death, love, memories, hopes and so on. Depending on the tamada each individual toast may amount to a rather long speech on the subject. Once the toast is finalized everyone around the table will exclaim: "*Gaumarjos!*" (literally: "Victory!"), and empty their glasses. Not emptying your glass, Beka instructs us, shows a lack of respect for the subject of the toast. There was seemingly no proper way of ending the drinking before Beka decided so.

Only much later did we realize that the very strict rules and norms around Beka's table were actually bendable in other settings and, later on, even when drinking with Beka. Depending on the participants and the occasion, the level of ritualization and rigidity of the supra differs. Generally speaking if there is access to some quantity of food, and most importantly drink, there is always a good reason to have a supra. However, our first experience with the supra was in the role of being foreign guests and Beka took it upon himself to be a strict tamada in order to teach us the proper ways of this proud Georgian tradition.

Analyses of the Georgian supra have rightly evolved around it being a vehicle of highly idealized socio-cultural communication and control. It has been engaged and analyzed in relation to themes such as excessive consumption and display,[3] second economies and manipulation of relations with the state during Soviet rule,[4] national, cultural and gender identity,[5] the invention and representation of tradition, and host-guest relations.[6] In that sense, it has traditionally within the literature been viewed as a secular ritual producing certainty about socio-cultural ideals, roles and categories. Through the evenings we spend with Beka's homemade wine and his mother-in-law's abundant repertoire of traditional Georgian dishes, we were educated not only in proper Georgian drinking but, more importantly, through Beka's elaborate toasting, in Georgian culture, history, tradition and life. Or, at least, the idealized versions of these. No mention is ever made of the turmoil of the nineties, nor the Soviet period preceding it. Talk and toasts evolve around the nation's traditional values, its glorious past and its promising future.

Stories of a winemaker

Besides being a winemaker and a master of giving toasts, Beka is a storyteller. As well as speaking about the history of his nation, he enthrals us with tales of his youth; bear hunts in the mountains, helping Chechen refugees on the Georgian-Chechen border, elaborate drinking parties, fights. One warm summer evening a small group of Beka's old friends have been gathered for a supra on the terrace outside the farmhouse. While plates of food are continuously piled up on the table and wineglasses filled and emptied, Beka recounts the story of an expedition in the mountains where he and some local friends had stumbled across Daniel – a Dutchman also present at the supra. "Daniel had been walking around for days in the mountains with no equipment at all", Beka laughs, "and in the evening he wrapped himself in cellophane instead of using a sleeping bag". Daniel smiles a bit and even though he seems to disagree somewhat with what is being told, he lets Beka continue. "Later, when I was already back in Tbilisi, he called me and said that he had been captured by some crazy people in a village and that they were forcing him to drink chacha all day long – I had to go and save him!"

Years later we will ourselves become part of Beka's stories, knowing at that point that they are not necessarily complete replicas of events as they took place. But also that this doesn't matter. They still convey an overall truth. One such story springs from this first visit. We join Beka on a trip to the city Telavi in the Kakheti region of eastern Georgia. Beka has a meeting there with some business partners, and while he is occupied we stroll around in the city. Not long into our walk we meet a young man who invites us to come to his house as his guests. More by force than by choice we go with him. The house is modest and, although he and his family have little to offer, a table of food and wine is soon prepared. Neighbours come and join our toasting and although Beka calls us several times to let us know that his meeting is over and we need to go back, our hosts refuse to let us go. Not until Beka comes to our rescue are we able to leave. We have been hostages as much as we have been guests. This, at least, is the story according to Beka.

To be sure, we were invited in by the young man, but in our memory it was merely for a cup of tea with him and his sister – an English teacher eager to take the rare opportunity to practice her language skills. The two showed us some pictures in a photo album, we exchanged email addresses, the young man gave us a cuddly toy as a present and we left. But this latter variety is not a very good story, certainly not compared to Beka's version. In the years to come other stories of our visits at Beka's house will appear; about the day a man from a nearby village brought a horse to the farmhouse so that Katrine could take a ride, and how the villager – as soon as Beka and Martin were out of sight – attempted to kidnap Katrine and bring her back to the village as his bride (heroically obstructed by Beka); and about the evening when Beka and Martin devoured 20 litres of his wine without barely becoming intoxicated. As with the story of the visit in Telavi, Beka's versions are slightly different from what we ourselves remember. But they still pertain to a certain reality; they relate to the cultural practice of bride-napping in rural regions of the country and the question of an aspect of masculinity residing in being able to drink massive quantities of wine, but never being intoxicated.[7] In this style of narration Beka is able not only to tell stories about our friendship but also to root our relations in a grander story of Georgia and Georgian traditions. And, at the same time, he is able to subtly relate to the ambivalence now and then felt towards these traditions (the moral quandaries of bride-napping, the obligations to host and be hosted, and the pressure to drink excessively) through humour and allegory rather than explicit discussion and argument.

Beka's way of storytelling is revealing in the sense that is shows public representation to be extremely important. As we will see in the chapters that follow, this is not only the case in relation to how individuals tell of themselves and their country, but also, and perhaps even more so, on the political level. It is furthermore revealing because it is an idealized version of something that *could be*, perhaps even *ought to be* – at least within a particular framework of thinking. It is not necessarily the truth value of the story that is important – most who are acquainted with Beka will probably know that it has been elaborated on – but rather the form and telling of a story in itself as well as what its content symbolizes and engages. On the level of ideal, his story about our trip to Telavi is one of an important cultural practice – hospitality – a practice that was severely challenged by the socio-economic detour large parts of the population suffered during the 1990s and still was at this point.[8] Beka could tell this story with confidence because he fitted well into it – it *could* have been a story about him which he would have no problems living up to.

The winemaker and the new president

Beka is excited about the revolution and the new political leader. He praises the revolution and the, in his opinion, much-needed change it will bring. Having been educated in the US, Saakashvili is a man of reforms, change and progress; of bold initiatives and extreme measures to fight corruption, lawlessness and organized crime. Contrary to Shevardnadze and his allies, Beka lets us know, Saakashvili is not stuck in the communist past and a Soviet mentality – nor dependent on corrupt networks to stay in power. He is a man of vision, and Beka seems certain that, from now on, initiative, talent and hard work will be rewarded. Something that is much-needed if Georgians are to rebuild their country and move forward. But Beka's accentuation of the positive qualities of Saakashvili's emphasis on initiative and hard work oddly contrasts with some of the main qualities he ascribes to the Georgian national character in general. "Georgian's are lazy", he often notes, continuing; "they don't really like to work but prefer to sit together and eat and drink". He tells the locally famous story of how, when God distributed land to the different nationalities of the world, the Georgians were not present because they were sitting somewhere else having a supra. When all land had been distributed and God finally found the Georgians he asked them why they had not stood in line like all the other nationalities. "We were drinking and making toasts in your honour", they replied him. And grateful over this, God gave them the land he had intended for himself. Georgians, according to Beka, adhere to proud cultural traditions. At the same time they are, in his own words, "lazy and crazy".

So how could this match Saakashvili and his visions of reform, initiative and hard work? It may have been because Saakashvili himself contained all these slightly ambiguous dualities. As mentioned in the introduction, Saakashvili had gained the nickname "crazy Misha" because of his forceful style and he had poetic qualities as a public speaker (not unlike those of a toastmaster). And, perhaps most importantly, despite his political agenda being one of progress and reform, he firmly drew on national, cultural history in his political practice. For instance, prior to his official inauguration, Saakashvili went to the Gelati monastery in Kutaisi and swore an oath by the tomb of King Davit the Builder. In the 12th century King Davit had partaken in uniting the Georgian nation and is considered one the greatest rulers in the nation's history. In the oath Saakashvili said that "Today Georgia is split and humiliated. We should unite to restore Georgia's territorial integrity. Georgia has existed and will exist. Georgia will become a united strong country."

Saakashvili's first act after the official ceremony, which took place a few days later, was to sign a decree that established a new state flag. The new flag, known as the Five Cross Flag, features five red crosses on a white background. It is said to originate from flags used in medieval Georgia by King Vakhtang Gorgasali and later by Queen Tamar – the great-granddaughter of King Davit the Builder – who ruled in a period known as the Georgian Golden Age where political union between kingdoms and principalities had been firmly established.[9] Many Georgians, including the influential Patriarch of the Orthodox Church, had supported the introduction of this flag already in the late nineties, but Shevardnadze had opposed it. Introducing it, Saakashvili not only distanced himself from the politics of Shevardnadze but also, with unmistakable symbolism, inserted his presidency in Georgian history. During the first months of his presidency, Saakashvili managed to turn towards the West and towards Georgia at the same time; he was both a modernizer and a traditionalist. Both these moves were moves away from Russia, the Soviet past and the chaos of the post-Soviet 1990s and towards promises of a future where the Georgian nation would be restored and rebuilt according to both cultural traditions and modern, democratic political practices. For a businessman and winemaker such as Beka, this was as ideal as it could be. Why should he not be optimistic?

Coda: Re-awakening and self-representations

The role of national (re)awakening has been a major theme in social scientific – and not least anthropological – studies of the post-Soviet region. The time immediately after the Rose Revolution in many respects parallels the time immediately after independence. And in many ways a similar analytical optic to that employed immediately after the fall of the Union may be employed to shed light on the vivid symbolism of the nation and its friends and foes made use of in relation to visions of future developments, as well as in the drawing of both its political and geographical borders. Both were times of optimism and both eras were heavily loaded with national symbolism and the drawing of boundaries to political predecessors: the Soviet Union and its perceived present political manifestation, Russia. And, in the case of Saakashvili: the chaotic and lawless 1990s, in particular Shevardnadze as a symbol of the continuation of essentially Soviet political practice.

Saakashvili's emphasis on national traditions and historical grandeur, however, was slightly different than that of the first president Zviad Gamsakhurdia. Besides referring to Georgian ethnicity and nationality as an *a priori* category of socio-cultural being, Saakashvili to a much larger extent than any of his predecessors emphasized how this pre-given identity was a source of unique features and qualities that could be nurtured in order to reach an even *higher* state of national *and modern* (in the sense of democratic, prosperous, civilized) perfection. In that sense, as we see exemplified in the portrait of Beka – a traditional winemaker and visionary businessman – the initial Rose Revolution imaginary embodied the potential of nurturing, displaying and representing unique national traditions while still initiating economic and political reforms ideologically aligned with (what were thought to be) Western lines of philosophy, progress and development.

Beka as an archetype of Georgian masculinity and tradition, combined with initiative and economic aspiration, amply illustrates why this duality of the project of Saakashvili and his close allies sat well among large segments of the population at the time. After all, when Saakashvili was formally elected president in early 2004 he was backed by more than 90 percent of the vote. Besides providing an alternative to a political practice that had effectively alienated much of the population over a ten-year period, it is highly likely that this duality of Saakashvili's revolutionary project broadened its appeal across the country. Part of its strength was the ability to encompass what from other perspectives may appear contradictory: highly traditionalist and nationalist aspirations – including the moral and cultural celebration of social obligations, kin, and the excessive displays of food, drink and leisure embodied in the supra and the tale of how the Georgian's got their land – and, simultaneously, the celebration of high-modernist, capitalist and neoliberal political philosophies, emphasizing free-market competition and individual responsibility, initiative and opportunity.

As we shall discuss further in the upcoming chapters, however, it may also have been this inherent duality that came to be the weakness of the revolutionary imaginary as daily life resumed and visionary promises had to translate into concrete policies, reforms and implementations. Just as initial optimism following the fall of the Soviet Union faded throughout the 1990s – not just in Georgia but across the region – so the optimism and euphoria in the wake of the Rose Revolution did not last through Saakashvili's first presidential term. Upon returning to Georgia in 2006 to conduct our first "proper" fieldworks, we would meet Marina; a woman who, at least at this point in time, approached and represented the revolution in very different terms than Beka. The portrait of her will be the vantage point of the following chapter.

Chapter 2

The Mother

Returning

It's now January 2006 and Georgia looks much different in its winter attire. The air is crisp and freezing cold; colder than usual people say – and there is more snow. Martin arrives in the middle of the night. He is to stay with Nina and Beka for a few days until he finds his own place to rent, this time staying in their Tbilisi apartment located in the Saburtalo neighbourhood. He takes one of the numerous pirate taxis at the airport and the elderly driver rushes towards the city centre. "*Dva!*" he triumphantly exclaims as they cross a red light for the second time. "No police", he laughs. He stops at a remote gas-station on the way, and Martin pays half of the fare so that the car can be filled up. The driver opens the tailboard and gasoline is poured into a hole located at some spot where the backseat used to be. He steps away to smoke a cigarette and a dizzying smell of gasoline soon engulfs the taxi.

Beka drowsily greets Martin as the taxi arrives in Saburtalo. It's four o'clock in the morning. Their apartment is located in a Soviet-style block, probably built in the 1960s. The elevator takes them up to the fifth floor, rumbling, squeaking, but working. "Saburtalo is the most comfortable neighbourhood in Tbilisi", Beka notes. "Foreigners always go to Old Town because it looks more exotic, but there is no heating there." Martin unloads his luggage by the couch in the living room. He and Beka share some bread and wine in the kitchen before going to bed for a few hours of extra sleep.

Both Nina and Beka are at work when Martin wakes up the next morning, and the kids are at school. This, and the following days, he wanders around in the neighbourhood or stays at home with Gulo who spends most of her time cooking. In the evenings

Nina and Martin look through local newspapers for a place to rent. Possibilities seem abundant as numerous families are renting out either rooms or entire apartments to foreigners in order to secure an extra income. But Nina is picky. Like Beka, she insists that we find something in Saburtalo or Vake but the ones they find are either too expensive or, in her opinion, too run down. Martin ends up staying with them for several days and celebrating Georgian New Year together with their extended family. During the feast everyone insists that it is worthless to talk about politics, yet everyone is talking about politics, constantly. One of the relatives note that "the new government is bla-bla-bla, but nothing really happens. But at least there is a possibility for change now – that was not the case in the Shevardnadze period." Another complains about the government selling the main electricity company to the Russians, creating a renewed dependence on Moscow. A third complains about the IDPs living in Tbilisi. A fourth that many of his friends have been fired from their public-sector jobs and replaced by young, unexperienced supporters of Saakashvili. Toasts and laughter continuously interchange with disagreements and shouting throughout the evening and the night.

A few days later Nina has more or less given up on the rent ads, and tells Martin that a friend of a friend of Gulo knows of an apartment in Mtatsminda, the neighbourhood just next to the Old Town. It's not Saburtalo or Vake, but she thinks it sounds good, although Martin will be staying with a local family instead of on his own. The price is 300 USD monthly for the room plus breakfast. Beka likes the idea, mainly because there will be someone there to make sure that Martin is fed. Reflecting ideals of gender roles and obligations, he thinks a man living on his own without someone to cook and clean for him sounds somewhat strange.

The family

Somewhere in Mtatsminda three generations of women are living together in an apartment located on the second floor of an old classical building. The second floor is actually shared by two families, each having their own kitchen and bath and different rooms along the long hallway that runs through the apartment. There are cracks here and there on walls and ceilings, signalling that it has been a while since any amendments have been carried out. Emma, the grandmother, is a pensioner, and Masha, the early-teen daughter, goes to school. Besides Emma's modest state pensions, Marina, the mother, is the single provider. She works two jobs but still finds it difficult to make ends meet. Prices are constantly on the rise and she is determined to send Masha to private classes for her to learn German and English. Sometimes the family is forced to sell an heirloom on the market to secure a steady income, but still, they have to live off a minimum. As a means to earn extra money Marina decides to rent out Masha's room, leaving the three women to sleep in the same bedroom. Emma dislikes the idea of having a complete stranger in the house – how can they know that this person will be trustworthy? What if something is broken or stolen, or rent is not paid? It should be a woman renting the room at least, perhaps a student, and definitely not a foreigner. Despite Emma's reservations, Marina places an advertisement in a local newspaper, announcing the room for rent, and lets people in her private network spread the news. Soon after, Martin comes by to see it. Emma's discontent is obvious on his first visit. While Marina smilingly and energetically shows him around, and Masha observes them with curious eyes from a safe distance, Emma ignores him completely. "We will be sharing our small kitchen", Marina says, "and you're free to use the balcony in the backyard – it's a traditional Georgian backyard, very beautiful during summer". After the tour Martin agrees to rent the room. Emma has not uttered a word.

When Martin moves his things to the apartment a few days later, only Emma is at home. She brings him to the kitchen, makes him sit down across from her at the table, and methodically begins pointing at everything in sight, stating the object's name in Georgian and encouraging him to repeat: *"khakhvi, k´art´opili, santeli, ch´ika, shakari, chai"*. As Martin, and later on also Katrine, soon learns, Emma's pedagogy in terms of teaching entails that if a word is not understood immediately she will repeat it again and again, louder and louder. Her look is stern. There is to be no doubt that he is there on her premises. She cannot hold back a smile however as she forces him to eat two raw cloves of garlic and in the end it is Emma who, upon seeing the contents of Martin's first bag of groceries brought to the kitchen, decides that he is to eat with them in the evening as well instead of preparing food alone. Not long after, Martin stays as a regular member of the family. "Emma says that you'll be as fat as me by the time you leave", Marina laughs. Emma notes that hopefully he will be less fat, as Marina eats too much. "Please excuse my mother", Marina laughs; "she talks a lot".

Power-cuts and other shortages

Days and evenings with the family soon come to follow a strict schedule; Marina and Martin have breakfast together in the morning before she goes to her first job of the day and he goes to the NGO office where he is carrying out his fieldwork. He returns around six in the evening and has dinner with Emma and Masha, Marina joining them a bit later after having finished at her second job. They usually have soup, white bread and tea with lemon. Emma and Marina then take turns talking on the telephone, which takes about an hour. At eight they all go to the living room to watch TV. Most often they watch Emma's favourite dubbed Mexican soap opera, but sometimes she allows Marina and Martin to watch the news. After a few hours of watching TV and a few more phone conversations, Marina will return to the kitchen to clean up and start cooking for the next day.

One evening when watching the news, they learn that there has been an explosion in North Ossetia: the Mozdok-Tbilisi gas-pipeline leading from Russia to Georgia has been sabotaged. Marina is relatively calm about it, and goes to the kitchen to fetch some pickled pumpkin for dessert. President Saakashvili, who appears on TV, is less calm and calls it a highly suspicious event. It turns out that there have actually been two explosions, as well as an act of sabotage against electricity lines many miles away. There might be enough reserves in Georgia for tomorrow but after that, the country potentially faces up to ten days without gas along with the already common power-cuts. Saakashvili remarks in a speech that this is a very organized action that has taken several hours to carry out and coordinate; "it happens at a moment where we are negotiating different possibilities", he says, referring to Georgia being in talks with both Western Europe and Azerbaijan about access to energy sources that will make Georgia less dependent on Russia. "How is it possible", he continues, "that it happens exactly now? The only thing that can stop the rapid development in Georgia is hitting on our gas supplies!" There is no doubt that he believes this to have been carried out by Russians, probably the authorities, as a means to put political pressure on Georgia. The Georgian leadership's explicit distancing to past alliances and Russian domination, as well as their aspirations towards NATO membership and political and military alliances with the US and EU, are arguable provocative and potentially threatening to Russia who still sees the former Soviet space, including Georgia, as her rightful sphere of influence.

The following day there is a power-cut in the evening. Emma and Martin eat by candlelight in the kitchen, wrapped in their coats. It's freezing cold inside and outside, the temperature is at a historic low. After a few hours electricity comes back; "the gift of life!" Emma says. It might disappear again at any given moment, so they go to watch TV while they can. There's footage of people standing in long lines trying to secure petrol. "We'll get through this, we've been standing in line many times before", a man sarcastically notes to a reporter. There is also footage of a small group of people in Tbilisi demonstrating against Russia. People carry signs reading "GasPutin". Emma does not understand why everyone is always against the Russians – personally she likes them, her brother lives in Russia along with other family members and friends, and she has fond memories of being there in the past. Her health, money and the current visa regulations all make it almost impossible to go there now. They have a glass of homemade cherry brandy to keep them warm, and soon after there is a power-cut again.

As Saturday arrives, Marina and Martin go on their weekly trip to *bazroba* – the main market in town – to shop for groceries. Prices on most goods have increased even more as a consequence of the gas shortage, and Marina is not able to buy the things she wanted. In the covered meat and fish market she goes back and forth between stalls, seeking out the best buys. She's tired of always eating soup and bread for dinner, but meat is expensive so often she has to settle on some of the cheaper cuts that few others want to purchase: some tongue, stomach or brains, or some small fish caught in local rivers. As Marina and Martin return home, Emma meticulously goes through all the bags, asking what was paid for each item. Regardless of Marina's efforts, everything is always deemed either too expensive or too excessive. And by the way they smoke too much, they are told. Nevertheless, as soon as Marina leaves to visit some friends, Emma sends Martin out to buy a beer or two for them to share – firmly denying it ever having happened once Marina returns.

The picture of Stalin

"We are Lenin's workers", Marina says and laughs. It's evening and dinner plates have been removed from the table in the kitchen. They're sitting amidst a wealth of walnuts. Marina and Martin have been given the assignment of cracking the nuts with small hammers on a breadboard so that Emma can remove contents from shells. "Lenin's project was a good idea but..." Marina pauses while shaking her head, "it just wasn't a very good idea in practice". Inadvertently she throws a handful of unsorted shells and nuts into the wrong bowl, the one containing discarded shells. *"Duda, duda!"* Emma laughs in a rusty voice. She begins to pick them up again so that nothing is lost. "Homo Sovieticus", Marina says, hinting to the fact that Emma mainly speaks in Russian rather than Georgian. Pieces of shell hit the ceiling and fall down around our heads. "Our guest is exploited for labour", Emma says in Russian and laughs. While peeling nuts Emma reminisces about her schooldays, while simultaneously scolding Martin for some mispronounced words in Georgian. "I was lazy in school as well", she says forgivingly while she shudders slightly in her turquoise-green duvet jacket. "But I was clever with my hands and good at being creative", she continues. Emma is now 85 years old and has experienced both the Soviet period and independence for good and bad. She was trained as an economist and before that she went to one of the numerous communist schools in which order and respect were central elements. Pictures of Stalin, who at that time was leader of the USSR, were hanging in all classrooms, and in her art class one of the assignments was to draw him. But during one such art class Emma didn't care to draw the entire portrait at once. So she divided the picture to be copied into small squares. "Then I cut my own piece of paper into squares as well and started painting them one by one", she explains with an arch smile. When little Emma finally reassembled the squares she had created a picture of Stalin that looked like a Picasso rendition of the Man of Steel. "Ooooh the trouble it caused", she laughs, "when my teachers found out that I had created a distorted Stalin". Marina and Emma fall back in their chairs laughing while Masha stands in the doorway smiling a little.

Emma goes on to reminisce how the Soviet period was a time of control and fear. Yet as an economist with a good job it was, in some ways, also a good period. Her husband was still alive then and she laughingly tells us stories of how evenings were spent with "cigarettes, beer and pool – I was excellent at playing pool". They would go out in the evening, travel during holidays and, in general, lead a good life. She rarely goes out now due to her bad health, cigarettes have been abandoned, officially also beer, and her memories are from a lost time. Now in 2006, pictures of Stalin are often only found at flea markets. Not least at the Dry Bridge Sunday market, but it is not only Soviet artefacts that are being sold; it is anything that can earn the seller a small, extra income. General economic stagnation since independence has meant that at this time over 30 percent of the general population lives in poverty. For people such as Marina it is not the past, but the present that needs attention. Although she's working two jobs, it is difficult to get by. With the prices on gasoline and groceries increasing, along with a steady flow of new taxes, there is an imminent threat of her having to sell the apartment, which has been home to the family for a long time. Marina might have lived through the final years of the Soviet Union, but it is the circumstances created by the last 15 years since independence that have framed her present-day life. The memories of Emma, "Homo Sovieticus", of the joys and sorrows present in her youth, are far removed from the reality Marina is in now. When Emma laughs at the fact that there is no longer a Stalin to cause problems, Marina laughs with her. But, Emma's stories are also reminders that everything did not turn out as it was thought to after the fall of the Soviet Union. For Marina, it is just as much the hopelessness of the present that she finds laughable. She doesn't feel there to be many possibilities for her to improve her own life; instead she aims at securing possibilities for Masha. On her part, Masha is part of the generation having come of age during independence, a generation for whom regional conflicts and social and political instability have always been part of everyday life. When Emma tells stories about Stalin the humorous aspect for Masha is to hear what her grandmother was like as a child, and not so much the Soviet period itself. Masha is more concerned about whether they will ever get a computer and some Internet access.

One morning during breakfast, Martin asks Marina whether they participated in the Rose Revolution; did they join the masses on the streets? They didn't. But since they are living close to the parliament building, they saw the crowds circling around it from their balcony. "They are good regisseurs, our American friends", she says, denoting the assistance Saakashvili had had from the US. She doesn't know whether the revolution was good or bad; "everybody wants to help themselves and not the people". She's not sure whether the revolution has really made a difference.

Life is a joke

By the summer of 2006, Katrine has taken over the room in the apartment. Again, living with the family means sharing the troubles, hopes and fears of its members; Marina's struggle to support the family economically, Emma's deteriorating health and Masha's schooling. Electricity cuts and gas shortages are discussed in the living room in front of the heater during winter or on the balcony during the intolerable heat of summer. Trips are taken to the market, to church and to family and friends, the cost of basic food items and the political turmoil of the country are debated over a game of *nardi*. The stories include memories of the repressive, though somewhat stable, Soviet rule; the hopes sparked by the gaining of independence in 1991; the following civil war; the hard-felt experiences of political instability and violence that marked both the country and the city during the nineties; the renewed hopes of change following the revolution; and the subsequent disappointments with the new government.

One evening in the spring of 2007, as we are both in Georgia and both staying with the family, we sit with Marina in the kitchen, secretly smoking and hoping not to be caught by Emma. Food for tomorrow is being prepared; we're having brains and tongue, a small feast in our honour. The mood however is all but festive. Marina has recently discovered that the family might be forced to leave their home. As part of a general beautification of the city, the municipality of Tbilisi along with the Ministry of Culture has announced that the neighbourhoods of Mtatsminda and Sololaki are to be rehabilitated. The majority of the renovation costs will be paid by the central government but a draft bill has proposed that the inhabitants are to partake in financing the project. The proposal suggests that every household is to pay a monthly tax between 10 tetri and 3 lari per square metre of their property. For Marina and her family the prospect of an extra expense is devastating. A likely outcome is that they will be forced to leave the apartment where both Marina and Masha have grown up and move into an even smaller apartment in the suburbs. We discuss their possibilities while Marina chops the meat for tomorrow. She fears how having to leave their home will affect Emma's health. She has a severe heart problem and, according to Marina, a change of address will end up killing her. Emma lives on her memories and these are intimately connected to the apartment and the life lived within it. Marina is obviously shaken by the situation.

"Our life is one big joke", she says, tears rolling down her cheeks; "we might as well sit back and laugh about it all". And, so we laugh together, in the midst of tears. "Maybe our Misha will help us", Marina continues, and we laugh even more, in the acknowledgement that he probably won't. At least from the point of view of Marina. The perceived progressiveness of the Rose Revolution government is laughable for Marina. In stating that their lives are one big joke, Marina does not intend to imply that this is a general feature and that it has always been so, but rather that at this specific moment life is becoming increasingly absurd. The realm of change for Marina at the time is not that of post-independence but that of post-revolution. The ambiguities and difficulties she and her family experience are largely results of the present moment.

Coda: Dispossession and disillusion

The statue Mother Georgia (*kartlis deda*) was erected in 1958 on the top of Sololaki hill overlooking the city, the year Tbilisi celebrated its 1500th anniversary. The 20-metre-tall aluminium statue is a figure of a woman wearing the Georgian national dress. She is meant to symbolize the Georgian national character: in her left hand she holds a bowl of wine to greet those who come as friends and in her right hand is a sword for those who come as enemies. The figure of the mother is important in Georgia; it is she who raises the new generation and she who prepares food and feasts for family and guests.[1]

Although it had been out of financial necessity rather than hospitality that Marina opened her home to us, and although Emma had perhaps initially been more inclined to put forth the sword and not the wine, they both ended up accepting and seeing us as their guests and later as their family. However, contrary to Beka and his family, they lacked the means to perform a traditional display of hospitality; the grand meals, the wine. They could simply not uphold this traditional representation of Georgia, nor, like Beka, tell stories situating themselves in an ideal position within it, but had instead to deal constantly with the small and large efforts and obstacles of keeping everyday life going. Marina could not dedicate her daily life to keeping house and nursing children, to cooking and caring for her family and guests while a husband provided the financial means for the household – as the archetypical gender and family ideals put forth in the cultural representations we saw in the previous chapter would have it. Apart from being a mother and caring for her family in the household, she also had to take on the role as a single provider for her family, constantly facing the challenge of making ends meet, and, hence, constantly experiencing her reality and capabilities standing in sharp contrast to the cultural and social ideals associated with Georgian family life. And she was not alone in having this experience. Indeed, poverty and social fragmentation had severely challenged thousands of Georgian families throughout the 1990s and up until this particular point in time.[2]

In her book *The Unmaking of Soviet Life*, the anthropologist Caroline Humphrey has used the notion of dispossession to describe a dual characteristic of certain groups and people in the post-Soviet Russian political economy. The dispossessed, she argues,

> are people who have been deprived of property, work, and entitlements, but we can also understand them as people who are themselves no longer possessed. That is, they are no longer inside the quasi-feudal corporations, the collective "domains," which confer a social status on their members.[3]

In many ways, the term captures part of the experience of families such as that of Emma, Marina and Masha. But for Marina and others, at this point in time, dispossession was not created merely by the "post-Soviet condition"; it was configured in tandem with a post-revolutionary condition.

Marina was part of a generation that had been both severely disappointed and financially challenged as Georgia gained independence. Their daily lives had been reshuffled by the transition to market capitalism, the reorganization of property and production, and the grave economic decline of the nineties. Most of our friends and interlocutors would continuously refer to this period as the "black nineties" and recall an absolute lack of state control and provision of goods and services. It was a time in which the country suffered from massive corruption, excessive crime rates and an extensive control of criminal gangs, combined with a severe lack of basic supplies such as gas, water and electricity. But somehow, at least when recalled in the post-Rose Revolution context, these challenges had been shared by all but a very few. In contrast, the present was a time in which some, such as Beka and his family, were able to live up to cultural as well as revolutionary representations and ideals, while others, such as Marina and her family, felt increasingly left out, or left behind. For a large number of Georgians, the promise that with the Rose Revolution, the period of transition was over and a time of national and cultural prosperity had come, did not correspond to the daily experience of struggling merely to stay afloat.

When Saakashvili appeared on the TV screen Marina would often exclaim, "Ah, here is our Misha – he's such a little boy!" Here was no reference to the positive masculine traits that had been promoted during and after the revolution: the strong, vibrant man with a good heart and soul. On the contrary, here was a boy who did not seem to know what he was doing. And, even if he did, he did nothing for Marina. As a single mother, she herself was the one who had to display strength – something the boyish president in her opinion did not do. In many of his speeches, Saakashvili had stood firm on the statement that the transitional period in Georgia was over.[4] However, for Marina this was not the case. And, she was not the only one who could not see herself – or was not seen – in the revolutionary visions of cultural victory, economic prosperity and general progress.

Chapter 3

The Misfits

Hotel Sakartvelo

(Melody: "Hotel California")

On a dark mountain highway,
Potholes everywhere.
Warm smell of cattle,
Rising up through the air.
Out ahead in the distance,
I saw a shimmering light,
I knew it was a mirage,
There ain't no power at night.
There he slouched in the doorway,
Cigarette in his hand, he said,
"Welcome to Sakartvelo,
Our beautiful land!"
Then he lit up a candle,
And gave it to me straight,
"To go through is twenty lari,
To go quick twenty-eight".

Welcome to the Hotel Sakartvelo!
Such a lovely place (such a lovely place),
Seen from far away!
They're living it up at the Hotel Sakartvelo!
What a nice surprise (what a nice surprise),
Bring your own supplies!

The electricity's twisted,
It's never ever online, and he said,

"We don't have no power here
Cause it's the spirit of the times".
How they drink in the courtyard,
The wine tastes of regret.
Some drink to remember,
I just want to forget!
So I called up the captain,
"Please bring me my wine", he said,
"We have had that spirit here since
BC four thousand and nine".
And still those hookers are calling from far away,
Wake you up in the middle of the night,
Just to hear them say:

Welcome to the Hotel Sakartvelo!
Cobwebs on the ceiling, can't get to my floor,
He said, "That's probably because the lift ain't working no more".
We have water problems, and there will be no light,
I said "You can bet your bottom dollar, my friend,
I won't be spending the night!"

Last thing I remember,
I was running for the door.
I had to find the passage back
To the place that I was before.
"Relax", said a policeman,
"It'll all be all right".
Couldn't get out of the country,
The planes all leave at midnight!

The lyrics to "Hotel Sakartvelo" (Hotel Georgia) were written by a group of expat teenagers living in Tbilisi because of their parents' jobs. At this time the expat community in the country was vast. There were a myriad of different international aid agencies, most of them based in Tbilisi, working with ethnic minorities, IDPs, poverty-struck families, orphans and other marginalized or underprivileged groups. Adding to this there were the equally numerous advisors and experts on good governance who had been brought in to assist the government in the post-revolutionary reform processes. As pointed out by the anthropologist Erin Koch, these were years in which the government "allocated many previously state responsibilities to international agencies and NGOs, setting the stage for dependency on foreign assistance under the umbrella of neoliberal free market reforms that emphasized privatization, state withdrawal and individualism".[1]

Although the lyrics to "Hotel Sakartvelo" were written as an ironic comment to the contemporary situation, not unlike the irony Marina would often express, they also highlight some of the problems many people continued to face in spite of the revolution: broken infrastructure, lack of electricity, corruption, scarcity and alcoholism. Having officially declared the transition period over, these were all images the government had to overcome in order to escape the stereotypical (yet often true) characterizations of Georgia as a failed post-Soviet state, and to show both local citizens and the world community that things were indeed changing. But some figures betrayed such visions of change.

Underground

The apartment of Emma, Marina and Masha is located a few streets up from Rustaveli Avenue, the main street of central Tbilisi. In-between staying with them, we live by ourselves in a rented apartment one street down from Rustaveli, towards the river. Crossing Rustaveli itself is almost impossible due to the fierce traffic speeding through the city centre, but a number of underground passageways lend safety to pedestrians. The underground passageway at the middle of Rustaveli is lively during the day. Gold is bought and sold by a small group of elderly ladies at one end, while at the other end a mother has left her youngest child to beg. In the middle small shops are crammed in side-by-side. Some vendors sell shoes, others sell office supplies and various trinkets, or pastries, or cigarettes. Residents of Tbilisi move through in a steady stream and there's a constant crowd. At night however only a few people use the underground as a passage. The hectic traffic on Rustaveli has died down, making it possible to cross the street in relative safety. And above ground it doesn't smell of urine. Below ground the shops have all closed and the beggars have gone home. Only one man is present in a dimly lit spot, standing with his flute and a small radio. Whenever we have to cross Rustaveli Avenue at night we use this particular underground to go and say hello to him. The flute immediately bursts into a jazzy and lively tune. We start dancing, partaking in a short performance in honour of the small number of people that pass by in the meantime. With some luck, at the end of the song a lari or two has entered the cap laying on the ground.

The flutist once played in a symphony orchestra but lost his job some years ago. Now he forms a gathering point of various street musicians who come by at random. One night while dancing a drugged young man joins us, bringing a two-litre bottle of beer that we share in plastic cups. After a lari has been put into the cap, we take a break from the performance. We talk about the upcoming concert with the artist Jamiroquai – one of the first major Western stars to perform in Tbilisi for a long time. The concert has received a great deal of media attention over the last days. But the price of one of the cheapest tickets is a staggering 300 lari – more than most people earn in a month. "The concert is tomorrow and I'm going", says the flutist, "now I only need another 299 lari and I have enough for the ticket!" He laughs, and his eyes sparkle.

On the street

We originally became acquainted with the flutist through Gia, one of our mutual friends whom we met one night in a bar a few months earlier. At this point in time, we spend most of our weekends with Gia and his friends Vanya and Misha, playing cards at our place, sitting in what becomes our regular café curing or working up a hangover, or engaging in "*birzha*". Birzha is a widespread phenomenon. It's what people – mainly young men – do when they have nothing else to do. They hang out on the street, walk around aimlessly, talk, mock-fight, sit in parks with a few bottles of beer, chain-smoke, pass time.[2]

Besides youth hanging out and passing time, other figures also attract attention in the city landscape. Unregistered street vendors are everywhere visible and include elderly women selling a handful of lemons or a few bundles of greens or flowers and others peddling vegetables, cigarettes, electronics, toys or homemade pastries on the staircases of the underground passages, in the periphery of the bazaars and in the bustling and crowded bus stations. Many others are constantly on the streets. There is the old blind man in the underground passage at Baratashvili Street who stands at the exact same spot almost without any movement for the entire day; there is the group of Roma girls roaming around in 9 April Park, either playing or attaching themselves firmly to the wrists of foreigners and not letting go before a lari or two has appeared; there is the middle-aged man with the large black beard who walks up and down Rustaveli Avenue with his daughter asking passer-bys for a coin; there is the line of old women standing in front of the Orthodox churches in Mtatsminda and Sololaki saying a prayer for a lari; there is the mother and her two young sons who sit on cardboard on Shavteli Street asking for money for a piece of bread.

They've all become a regular part of urban space in central Tbilisi. The locals know them. Some stop to chat, some regularly give them small change if they have something to spare, while others have learned to ignore them. In the afternoon they all leave. Katrine's father visits us at some point and he also quickly comes to recognize them. One day he spots one of the ladies who usually stands on Shavteli Street and offers her some coins, but she kindly declines them as she's "no longer at work". At night a different group of people appears, such as the flutist at Rustaveli, and small groups of boys who are inclined to take rather than beg for money.

Sudden unemployment, lack of state support, unresolved territorial conflicts and processes of dispossession as those described in the previous chapter all form a backdrop for this scenery. While some individuals and families manage to survive through extra jobs, selling items of value, receiving remittances from relatives living abroad, renting out apartments, or turning their car into a pirate taxi, other have been even less fortunate. New-comers to the streets are easy to recognize. Their faces are usually hidden, covered by a hand or a piece of cloth. They have a small sign asking for help so that they don't have to constantly say it, clinging on to at least some sense of pride. They are often elderly people with no possibilities of getting a job, or single parents who are desperate to feed their children.

A toast to Mr. President

Struggling to get by is a widespread phenomenon. Gia, the young man who had introduced us to the flutist, has himself struggled for much of his life, as have many of his friends. Most of them now work random jobs, often in relation to the oil pipeline that is being constructed in the region. But prospects are continuously bleak. Most weekends are spent supressing this bleakness by having fun either on the street or in a bar. The places we visit are almost living stereotypes; a basement bar where a disengaged lounge singer in a red dress works her way through a set of Russian songs that she has undoubtedly worked through hundreds of times before, accompanied by an elderly man on an electric keyboard who is equally disengaged in the performance and never looks up; dim lighting; assortments of cheap but good Russian and Georgian food; assortments of vodka and champagne, and local wine served by the litre; The Beatles being played on the stereo as soon as the lounge singer finishes her set. Gia often claims to be the biggest Beatles fan in the Caucasus and he meticulously takes us through their entire repertoire during the long evenings and nights we spend either in one of the regular bars, at our place or in his own apartment. He lives in the latter with his wife and their young daughter, both of whom often join us. He once had dreams of becoming a musician himself, but an injury prevented him from playing the guitar for a period of time and he now has to take care of his family, so those dreams have been shelved. But music still matters. When we're at the bar Ameron's, Beatles music is almost always played as we are often the only customers present so Gia has full access to the stereo behind the bar. At Afrodite the hostess usually provides the entertainment herself, jumping behind the piano and encouraging guests to sing and dance whenever the mood in the place becomes too sombre. Both places, however, are soon to disappear. New taxes and new competing "European-style" cafés opening by the dozen mean that many of the waterholes frequented by the post-Soviet generation of Gia and his friends are closing. This is unsurprising, perhaps, as we are constantly told by politicians that the post-Soviet times are over.

Despite knowing – or perhaps because of knowing – that many of these places are soon to be gone, we all have fun, singing, talking, killing hangovers with champagne, making toasts to love, music and flowers, and carrying each other home through the dark streets whenever someone has had too much for too long. But there is always an imminent sense that something seems to be coming to an end, which is only reinforced by the fact that many of the people in our small group are planning to leave, hoping that migrating to another country will make it possible to live a better life, to use one's education or get an education. Whenever we talk about the dire situation still faced by many Georgians, someone raises a glass with their left hand and announces a toast to "Mr. President" – playing on the local notion that a toast is only sincere when given with the right hand. There is thus often a mockery of the situation similar to the one found in the lyrics of "Hotel Sakartvelo"; comments on the pot-holed roads, the power-cuts and the corrupt officials, and an annoyance that the changes taking place seem to entail the disappearance of the good parts of this world, rather than the bad ones.

So at present, our small group of friends are not living the lives they had hoped for; but at least they have survived, at least their struggles have meant that none of them have ended on the street. One afternoon we are sitting in a café on Rustaveli with Gia, Vanya, Misha and a few others. A child enters from the street and goes from table to table begging for money. As he comes to us one of the guys tells him off, saying he'll get nothing from here. The episode sparks a discussion of whether or not to give a few coins to the many begging children like this one. Gia argues that one thing is giving money to one of the elderly people standing in the streets, or even to the flutist who has fallen into depression and alcoholism after being fired from his job in the orchestra. With the children it is something else. They are young and healthy and can work for themselves; giving them money will just get them used to lazily roaming the streets instead of working for a living, Gia notes. When he himself was a pre-teenager he was working, moving around heavy loads of goods at a marketplace in Turkey. It was tough, but he survived and it taught him how to take care of himself and not expect others to do it for him. Children like these could, and should, do the same. Or get help from one of the many NGO-run projects dealing with these issues.

Sparrows

But reality for many children is somewhat different now compared to when Gia was young. Due to scarcity, and the inability to buy food and vital medicines, many parents have been forced to give up one or several children in order to survive themselves and take care of their remaining offspring.[3] Some parents simply abandon their children in shops, at markets or by railway stations. Others attempt to sell them either as labour or as organ donors. Some children are sent out to beg and return only to find their family has left. Others again have parents who are imprisoned, and yet another group has ended on the street by their own choice as a means to escape abusive parents or relatives. Day shelters, night shelters, institutions and orphanages have all grown in number. Some are supported by local volunteers and charity organizations, but most by international NGOs and donor agencies. At this time there are around 5000 children placed in various kinds of institutions and centres throughout the country, many of them in Tbilisi. Around 90 percent have at least one parent meaning that they have either run away, been thrown out, or been abandoned. Added to this are the approximately 850 children living permanently on the street.[4]

The NGO in which Martin is conducting fieldwork is a centre for psychosocial aid and they regularly cooperate with organizations that run shelters and centres for at-risk children and youth. One of these is a day and night shelter called "Sparrows". It is located in the outskirts of Old Town in an old two-storey house surrounded by a broken brick wall. The building is patched with pieces of tin and wood and it houses around 50 children aged five to sixteen. The building was donated to the project by the previous government back in 1997, but it no longer receives any public support and is instead kept going through international donors. Keti is the project manager of the NGO that runs the shelter. Martin regularly meets with her and she explains that the children often experience problems with both police and the surrounding society, and there are problems related to drug use (primarily glue; regular drugs are not difficult to find but they are too expensive). But the most pertinent problem for the children in shelters such as this one is that once they reach a certain age they'll have to leave. "It's a real problem", Keti says at one point:

> We've always had this; ever since we started our activities this has been a serious problem because even people who have an education can't find a job, and what to do with these children who are poorly educated and have bad social habits? The goal is to have these children overcome their problems and to grow up, and when they are sixteen let other organizations help them, but ten years have passed and nobody shows any wish to help them. Many say they will employ them but nobody can employ them because unemployment is a very big problem in Georgia and it doesn't decrease, it still exists just as it was ten years ago and fifteen years ago and now maybe it's worse. And you know, the children feel this, they realize this, and they become nervous... we have very serious problems with them because they don't know what to do or where to go. In the centre they have a good environment, they have other children, and educators who help them. But when they leave the centre they have to leave them independently and to earn money, which is impossible now in Georgia.

Statistics confirm Keti's statement. The unemployment rate in the country grew steadily from 11.1 percent in 2001 to 13.8 percent in 2005. In the first quarter of 2006 it had further increased to 14.6 percent. The age group experiencing the highest percentage of unemployment in 2005 was those between the ages of 15 and 24 where the rate amounted to 28.3 percent.[5] The youths leaving the centres unprotected are thus left with meagre opportunities; their educational and social backgrounds are usually inferior compared with much of the remaining population. And so they often end up exactly where they came from: the streets.

And once on the streets, the children and youths are difficult to ignore. They don't blend in as well as the blind beggar who stands completely still at the same spot in the underground passage or the women in front of churches. Instead, they are noisy, they roam around, they sneak into restaurants and cafés to beg before they're thrown out. Some are pickpockets and they seem to be growing in numbers.

Reform, reform, reform

> The government seems to be thinking that they will develop a terribly hard-core economy and they will worry about social issues later, and the anecdote goes "if there will be anybody left to benefit from them". (Tamuna, project director of an international NGO)

The first years following the revolution are years of reform. However, even if the many reforms are put forth by the government as an illustration of the speed and profundity of change following the revolution, critical voices point out that perhaps the number of reforms is not itself an indication of change for the better. For instance, one local NGO worker notes that the government seems to be a little too inclined to adopt new reforms, laws and regulations, but there is never really any clear plan about how these are to implemented, which means that they often aren't.[6] And if they are, the outcome is not by definition a good change for all; sometimes new reforms are even mutually exclusive.

The majority of reforms are aimed at boosting economic development and modernization, but effectively they often also mean a further marginalization of already marginal and struggling groups. For instance, reflecting an ambition to privatize and modernize, make streets and public space appear neater, and inhibit unregulated trade, laws aimed at eliminating small-scale street trade are passed. This results in the closing-down of unauthorized outdoor bazaars and the criminalization of one of the most common sources of extra income for IDPs, pensioners and others with no formal employment, making people even more dependent on a system of humanitarian and social aid that has at this point largely been removed from government responsibility and taken over by international donor agencies and local NGOs.[7]

Commenting on the human consequences of recent reforms and prospects for future developments, Nino, another local NGO worker, reflects:

> I don't think that the whole nation, or at least the people who are in front of moving the society, have a clear vision of what we're planning to achieve in future years. A concept like a democratic country – whatever they say – we hear it but nobody really knows what it means. Freedom, respect of the law, tolerance... We don't know. Sometimes I think that this lack of a shared vision for the future years affects our present because we cannot unify, we cannot work together towards this objective.

The bleak characterizations given by Nino are a stark contrast to the revolutionary visions put forth by the government, epitomized in the number of reforms. In spite of abstract visions for the future taking a prominent place in government discourse,[8] to people like Nino these visions are unclear and do not manifest themselves in unification or shared objectives to work towards. Based on her experience of the reality she works in, they hardly result in a desirable future for all. Continuing the conversation, Martin asks: "How does it affect you having a government that makes a lot of promises and says this and that will happen, and..." Nino interrupts him:

> ...and then nothing happens? We are just disappointed, we are just... we cannot respect them and then you lose belief. And then you say that you know no government is supposed to serve their own interest. And then you are saying that politics is a dirty game and they never held their promises. So it means alienation from participation in this true civil society life and then you just fall back. They never do anything good for the people, everything is show-off and everything is PR and then you kind of keep your own way... and the government keeps to itself. So there is a gap and not really involvement – which is not good for Georgian advancement.

Martin asks Nino what she thinks will have changed by next year, and she replies:

> Hmmm... I think nothing... [she laughs a little]. Maybe some of us will be more desperate... [laughs loudly]. Those who still have hope [in a serious tone]... I don't think that during that time very big things will change, maybe small minor ones and we should learn to be happy about those minor changes also... But then when you have grown a little older Martin and you will come after ten years and we will have some changes.

Coda: Displacement and disappearance

There were vagrants and homeless people in Soviet times as well, but these had been removed on criminal charges. In the Soviet Union, they had been called "misfits" – they contradicted the official ideals of the working Soviet citizen.[9] In Tbilisi, and Georgia at large, contemporary misfits were also a visual contradiction. As we will discuss in more detail in the following chapter, the city centre of Tbilisi was an important arena for displaying the successes of modernization and development following the revolution. This meant that figures such as the flutist, the elderly beggars, street children, as well as the IDP population that very visibly were living cramped together in dilapidated former Soviet hotels in the central parts of the city, were all visual reminders to locals as well as foreigners of the shortcomings of government reforms and the non-fulfilled promises of the revolution. They were symbols of continuing social fragmentation, poverty, scarcity and the failure to resolve the territorial disputes in Abkhazia and South Ossetia. To paraphrase Erin Koch, the government approach to this problem largely became one of "displacing the displaced", and, we may add, the otherwise dispossessed.[10] That is, of removing them from sight as well as state responsibility.

Just as was the case with Nino above, a number of the people we spoke to in this period about the dire social problems facing the country actually acknowledged that things take time and that one could not expect everything to change overnight. However, this did not sit well with images of revolutionary change and promises that the transition period was over and a prosperous time had already come. When reviewing the government reforms and discourse of this period it was evidently a clear goal that changes had to be swift and overarching – revolutionary.[11] But paradoxically, exactly because of this urge to revolutionize, speed up processes, "disappear" social problems and break negative and stereotypical images such as those exemplified in the lyrics of "Hotel Sakartvelo", the reforms and developments came to produce, in some respects and particularly for the misfits, the reverse. Besides the efforts made to physically displace them from public view, the displacement of the social factors producing their situations from the realm of state responsibility onto international donors and aid agencies in many ways added to the problems rather than solving them. And the presence of the international NGO sector was itself a somewhat problematic issue as it served as a reminder that there were numerous issues the government could not take care of itself. Hence, when people such as Gia talked about the issue of street children it was evident that they did not expect the government to handle the situation. The revolutionary aspirations in some respects caused a reverse reality – one that was recognized and criticized by a growing number of locals as well as internationals. Things were indeed changing, but not necessarily for the better. In this sense, there was a growing pressure on the government to showcase that some things were actually being done. Which they did.

Chapter 4

The Pastel Shade

Surface politics

By 2007 the flutist below Rustaveli Avenue had disappeared, and along with him many other familiar street-figures of central Tbilisi, and a range of public spaces were being reconstructed in a peculiar mix of modernist architecture and traditionalist symbolism. Underground passages were emptied and shined-up with images of Georgia's ancient past on the walls; facades of old Tbilisi houses with wooden balconies were being painted in a range of pastel shades and many of the centrally located streets in the Old Town were being repaved. New statues appeared, such as the 35-metre-high granite and gold monument to Saint George in the city's central Freedom Square. The largest religious building in the region, the Sameba Cathedral funded by the secretive philanthropist billionaire Bidzina Ivanishvili, was standing as a new landmark on the left embankment reminding onlookers of the historical position and power of the Orthodox Church. These changes were becoming very noticeable in 2007, but the visual changes of Tbilisi had in fact already been initiated shortly after the revolution.

The first major wave of reconstructions had taken place already in early 2005 as a preparation for the visit of then-US president George W. Bush in May of that year. It was an important event for government as it symbolized the strengthened political ties with the US. Yet, among some parts of the population there was an inherent dissatisfaction towards the new political allegiance with the West. The most dramatic outcome of this dissatisfaction occurred on May 10th, when President Bush, along with Saakashvili, was giving a speech in Tbilisi in front of a crowd of 100,000 people on a podium at

Freedom Square. During Bush's speech a grenade was tossed from somewhere in the crowd towards the two presidents. It was the only assassination attempt of Bush during his presidency and it received a surprisingly sparse amount attention, mainly because it was immediately assumed that the grenade had been a dummy – it had not been a real assassination attempt but just a random madman throwing a disarmed Soviet war relic. Yet, in the days after the occurrence, as the perpetrator Vladimir Arutyunian was arrested and the grenade further examined, it was discovered that it had not been a dummy after all; it had actually been in perfect working order but miraculously did not detonate as the handkerchief it was wrapped in had somehow prevented the striker lever from releasing.

Arutyunian later reported that he had carried out the assassination attempt because he thought Georgia had become a puppet of the US. However, the public discontent surrounding President Bush's time in Georgia was generally much less dramatic and it was rarely directed towards the political aspect of the visit. Rather, it was directed towards what had been done as part of the preparations for the event. These preparations largely consisted of renovating the parts of Tbilisi that President Bush was going to see, and as he was not going to enter every building on his way, it was only the facades that were being renovated. While changes were thus on the one hand visible – something many people had longed for – they were also highly superficial, which was obvious to anyone stepping away from the route Bush was going to follow. Even Beka, who up until then had been a firm supporter of Saakashvili, remarked at one point while driving along one of the "Bush stretches" that "well, at least the painters have a job now", and many people drew parallels to the displays and renovations that had often been undertaken in Soviet times when the regime received foreign guests who were to be impressed, while more problematic issues were kept out of sight.

A few months after the presidential visit, city officials in

Tbilisi voted to rename the road leading from the airport to the city centre, which President Bush's motorcade had driven on during his stay, and call it "George Bush Street". A massive banner had actually already proclaimed the new name even before the vote took place, and despite protests from opposition lawmakers, then-mayor of Tbilisi Gigi Ugulava explained that "George Bush is doing a lot for the development of democracy in the world and is helping Georgia with its democratic transformation. And we are proud that one of Tbilisi's streets will carry his name."[1] Saakashvili himself was also quick to dismantle the critical views on reconstructions, stating in an interview on the subject that: "after President Bush leaves, I will take a brush in my hand and show that this façade painting is a continuous process".[2] And indeed it was. This chapter portrays the use of pastel shade in facade renovations not only in Tbilisi but also in other cities and villages, not least the village-cum-tourist attraction Sighnaghi. The process of painting facades, which locally came to be known "Sighnaghization", would later become a main trope of critique towards the government for conducting "surface politics". That is, a mode of politics based on creating exterior and superficial change while leaving insides – and thus the heart of problems – unchanged.

Tbilisi is a different country

So we are going to leave Tbilisi for a while. At this point in time doing so was, although in no way impossible, not necessarily a straightforward thing to do. And while people we knew in Tbilisi would continuously praise various places throughout the country that were worth a visit – the mountains to the north, the wine country to the east, the forested spa resorts to the south and the subtropical beaches to the west – they would often also suggest taking one-day trips whenever possible and returning again to Tbilisi. The primary explanation given was that finding a place to stay outside the capital could be difficult.

There had been relatively few tourists in the country after 1991. A main factor that withheld people from coming was the continuous political instability of the 1990s. Another, related, factor was the lack of tourist infrastructure. As in other Soviet republics, hotels in Georgia had largely been "Intourist" facilities; the official state travel agency of the Soviet Union, which had been founded by Stalin back in 1929. Georgia had in fact been a hotspot for tourism in Soviet times, not least among party officials who had flocked to spa resorts and impressive dachas along the coastline. But with the outbreak of war in Abkhazia and South Ossetia in the 1990s, almost every major hotel in the country had been used to house IDPs. Despite this, it was still possible to travel around the countryside, which we did on several occasions during our first years of coming to Georgia. A number of small homestays had opened, run by entrepreneur families such as that of Beka and Nina. But by and large finding a place to stay outside Tbilisi was a bit of a gamble; there were guidebooks but many places seemed to have closed in-between the authors' visits and the printing of the books.

In the summer of 2004 we go to Akhaltsikhe, a small town in the Samtskhe-Javakheti region in southern Georgia renowned for nearby cave city Vardzia, built in the slopes of Erusheti Mountain in the 12th century. We go there in a crammed *marshutka* (minibus) only to discover that there is nowhere in town to stay. Three hotels are mentioned in our guidebook but as we go to the addresses mentioned we find the first two to be closed, and in the third there is simply no one around despite the door being open. Going back to the bus station we also find that there won't be any marshutkas going back to Tbilisi until the following day. We are stuck. After a period of grumbling over possibilities we start walking randomly around and at one point we stumble into a local man who had also been on the marshutka from Tbilisi. He takes us to a nearby bank in order to ask people there whether any of them know either of any alternative hotels or other options of getting away. There are none. But after a while he manages to convince Nanuli, one of the female clerks, to let us stay in her house for a small fee. In her lunch break she brings us to her apartment, where she makes tea, cuts watermelon for us and finds a nardi game that can occupy us while she goes back to the bank to work for a few hours. She forgets, however, to tell her 20-year-old son about the arrangement, so he is mildly surprised as he enters the apartment to find two foreigners sitting in the living room. His name is Giorgi, we have some wine, and all turns out well.

In the summer of 2005 Martin and his girlfriend visit the city of Borjomi, heralded for its numerous natural springs and the site of several old spas and resorts. Yet despite the help of Beka's younger brother Temo, who has taken them there by car, it is impossible to find a hotel. The only place available is a vacant room in an old hotel that houses IDPs. There are dark wooden panels and marble floors everywhere, but with the groups of children playing and groups of men watching newcomers, it feels more like stepping into an indoor village than stepping into a hotel. It takes a while before someone comes to the reception, and although they never manage to figure out whether it is actually an employee or simply a random resident seeing an opportunity, they get a room. Temo is reluctant to let them stay there, but they insist that it is fine. A guidebook describes the place as safe and pleasant, with rooms that are "typically Soviet, with unappealing but functional bathrooms and temperamental electricity supply" – correct on all accounts. The room bears traces of former glory and present decay; fancy but torn tapestry, heavy but moth-eaten curtains, a beautiful marble bathtub with a drainage that appears to have been blocked for quite some time. Linens scratch, but there are beds and one can sleep.

In the spring of 2006 we decide to take a trip to Kazbegi, a mountain town in the Great Caucasus on the Georgian Military Highway close to Russia. There are allegedly numerous homestays to find, but the employees at the NGO where Martin works at the time insist that we make arrangements in advance. One employee has distant relatives there and they have a room for rent. We're told that once we arrive we have to walk by the stretch of street vendors next to the marshutka stop, turn left and go three streets up, turn right and then shout for Vato – he, or someone who knows him, will then come and find us. It works perfectly. In the evening we eat with Vato, his elderly mother and one of his friends. Vato, we soon learn, is very fond of vodka and cognac, and very fond of taking roadtrips in his old car along the mountain gorges afterwards.

In 2007 we go to the countryside the way most locals do – by going to a dacha or old family house in a village. It is Vanya, one of the young men described in the previous chapter, who invites us to go there with some of his other friends. We go by train to his mother's dacha, which is located in inner Kartli, about a one-hour drive from Tbilisi. We jump off the train in what seems to be the middle of nowhere and walk across a series of fields until we reach a small gathering of wooden houses in different shapes and sizes, all surrounded by a small garden. As we arrive Vanya's mother is busy drying apricots outside the cottage and she greets us warmly in Russian. We spend the day swimming in the nearby river and talk and sing on the vine-covered porch late into the night, with Vanya taking tours in the area now and then in search of homemade brandy among the neighbours.

Although there could not have been a better way of getting to know the country, these forms of travelling were not the kind of tourism that the government wanted to establish – not least because they were presumed not to attract the right kind of tourists, namely those with money to spend. And, even though hospitality surely epitomized our roaming through the country, the representational work in promoting the tradition of hospitality was difficult to achieve if there were no obvious places for visitors to stay. Therefore, a reconstruction program was established in order to renovate and construct tourist infrastructure in chosen sites and cities.

The brush of Saakashvili

Sighnaghi is a small town situated in the Kakheti region in eastern Georgia. It is located on a small hill overlooking a valley and facing the Greater Caucasus Mountains. Many of its oldest buildings date back to 1752 and were erected by King Heraclius II, but the town mainly grew during the Soviet period when it became an important agricultural centre for the surrounding fruit-growing region. Despite this, the population is only a little over 2000 people. Although thus being one of Georgia's smaller towns, Sighnaghi became a significant part of the reconstruction program initiated by the government seeking to turn it into a centre for the developing tourism industry – not least due to its picturesque location and the number of historical cultural sites in its vicinity. A few kilometres outside the town, we find for instance the newly restored Bodbe Monastery, which is a popular spot for Orthodox pilgrimage and an important symbol of the historical roots of Georgian Christianity. According to the legend, Saint Nino, a simple girl from Cappadocia, had a revelation in which the Virgin Mary told her to go to Kartli[3] and convert the people to Christianity. Against all odds, she succeeded in travelling the long distance by herself and later, by a miracle, she convinced King Miriam and Queen Nana to adopt Christianity as the state religion, making Georgia the first Christian state in the year 326 AC. Having accomplished her mission she went to the Bodbe gorge in Kahketi, where she later died, and King Miriam built a small monastery in her honour on the place where she was buried. The monastery had been turned into a hospital during the Soviet era but resumed its function as a convent after Georgian independence. The Bodbe Monastery and similar cultural and religious sites dating back to a glorious national past before Russian and Soviet rule, and the town's location in the main wine-producing region of Georgia, thus made it highly suitable for branding Georgian national heritage and character and attract foreign tourists.

As reconstruction projects began they fundamentally altered the town. "Sighnaghi is the most beautiful city in Europe", Saakashvili noted during an event where the renovation of the city was presented, continuing: "Neither Chinese, nor Americans, nor Turkish people can build the houses so fast, with such high quality and enthusiasm, like we did".[4] And the renovation and reconstruction of Sighnaghi certainly happened quickly. But many worried about the inadequacy of what was taking place. Not only did the work being done seem to solely to be aimed at turning the historic town into a tourist district rather than also restoring it for its residents, the methods used did not always follow common standards of renovation. That is, wooden windows would in some places be substituted with plastic ones, and houses would receive colours that they had never had before. Hence, as with the "George Bush stretch" in Tbilisi, the reconstruction of Sighnaghi had a superficial character in that it focused on exteriors rather than interiors, which was why the project paved way for the notion of Sighnaghization – referring to the process of Brusselization, known in urban planning as a question of haphazard urban development and redevelopment, and a laissez-faire attitude from authorities towards city planning.

As promised after President Bush's visit, Saakashvili had indeed swung his brush throughout Georgia, giving a completely new meaning to the notion of a colour revolution. Any city or village with a historic quarter (or a tourist-site) had received a layer of paint; Tbilisi, Kutaisi, Batumi, Telavi, Sighnaghi and Akhaltsikhe were all Sighnaghified (or "Disneyfied", as some also jokingly called it). But however far the pastel shade spread in the country and however much its proposed positive effects on the tourism sector were promoted by officials, there were still some who were highly critical of such measures – not least those living in the newly painted houses.

Pastel, Potemkin and facade-democracy

It is held that the Russian Minister Grigory Potemkin erected fake settlements along the banks of Dnieper River in order to impress (or fool) Empress Catherine the Great during her visit to Crimea in 1787. Potemkin villages are themselves held to be a historical fiction rather than a fact.[5] In Georgia, only a few years after the revolution, the myth of Potemkin became an image of a government seeking to create a myth about its own success through renovation projects taking place in Sighnaghi, Batumi and Tbilisi. The political opposition was among those who continuously blamed the government of Potemkin-like practices. But also local and international NGOs and human-rights groups observed that daily life for residents in places such as Sighnaghi had not improved. On the contrary, for many it had in fact become dangerous. For instance, a construction company, aptly called "Color", was responsible for removing the roofs of houses in three streets in Sighnaghi and covering them with ceramic tiles. However, this ended up damaging several of the houses. One resident, interviewed by a local human-rights organization, noted how "my house is in fact pulling down. The water is leaking from the ceramic plates. The walls are damaged; the floor is damp and the rooms got moldy." Other residents stated that there were afraid to let their children walk alone on the streets due to electricity wires lying on the streets and sewage wells left without lids.[6] There was a widespread opinion that reconstructions represented a desire not so much to renovate as to *be seen* renovating.[7]

In Tbilisi a similar process had started. It was no longer just the "George Bush stretch" that had been painted, but several other places as well, particularly in the city centre. As we mentioned in the previous chapter, in the home of Masha, Marina and Emma, the process of gentrification was of some concern.

Although Marina personally wanted to sell the apartment and find a smaller place in a nearby neighbourhood it was not the right time to do so. As previously mentioned she feared that moving might end up killing Emma. But Marina also feared that the question of staying or leaving might not be for her to decide at all. In other places of the Old Town residents were rumoured to being forcefully evicted in order to pave way for reconstructions.[8] Marina was afraid that this might also happen in her own neighbourhood as it, in her words, was "one of the neighbourhoods Misha likes", and that this was not always a good thing. Her apartment, along with the house in its entirety, unquestionably needed renovation, both outside and inside. In the living room a giant crack in one of the top corners of the room grew larger each time we visited. "I no longer have a president", she said at this time. Surely, Georgia might have become an easier country to travel in, but it had certainly not become an easier country to live in for all, regardless of ever-more-colourful facades.

Coda: Iconoclasm and palimpsests

During the Soviet period Freedom Square, where President Bush had held his speech and almost got assassinated, had been renamed twice, first becoming Beria Square[9] and later Lenin Square. In August 1991 the statue of Lenin residing in the middle of the square had been torn down, and the square once again came to be named Freedom Square. In November 2006 the golden statue of Saint George slaying the dragon, "The Liberty Monument", was unveiled, putting a final nail in the coffin of any symbolic reference to the Soviet Union. Such a process of iconoclasm was in no way unique to Georgia. The toppling of Lenin and Stalin statues had been almost standard procedure in many other former Soviet republics in attempts to re-signify public spaces and imbuing them with new meanings and values appropriate for new political narratives and ideals of national independence.

The idiom of iconoclasm, and political measures to symbolically overwrite the past through material reconstruction, has been a much-used trope in anthropological studies seeking to understand socio-political changes in the post-Soviet region, and the ways in which politicians and citizens tried to rid the present from the past.[10] It is noteworthy that the painting of facades entailed a paradoxical recycling of a practice that had taken place only a few years earlier. Serguei Oushakine, writing from a Russian context, has used the notion of post-socialist palimpsest to describe the process by which locals and officials alike attempted to overwrite or "hide" signs of the Soviet period.[11] In architectural terms, a palimpsest is figurative accumulation of different designs over time; rebuilt or remodelled spaces where traces of what has been covered remain. Along with iconoclasm, such new layers were much used in the post-Soviet space, for instance to invoke the coming of capitalism by showcasing individualized material additions to Soviet blocs, such as balconies, and thereby highlight new property rights. In post-revolutionary Tbilisi there were now post-post-socialist palimpsests emerging, or palimpsests squared; not only was the Soviet period covered or "disappeared", so was the post-Soviet period and the aspects of this period of time that did not fit current ideals, such as the misfits described in the previous chapter. Yet while iconoclasm effectively demolishes and removes something completely, palimpsests continue to showcase something of that which has been covered – it is a "not-quite" or a partial alteration.

"Colouring" in many ways followed this particular trajectory in that the greyness symbolically (and often stereotypically) associated with the Eastern Bloc was substituted with all the colours of the rainbow appearing on public and private buildings alike, along with neon lighting up cities at night, as countries gained independence.[12] But in many cases, just below this new layer of paint, life was more or less the same. Krisztina Fehérváry notes from the Hungarian context how the colour grey was seen as a representation of "life within a dark Iron Curtain, of enforced poverty and the fatigue of daily provisioning, of unsmiling salesclerks, scarce goods, and the lack of colourful advertising and commerce",[13] entailing that qualities of grey came to signify state socialism while capitalism was associated with colour. Saakashvili himself had allegedly been inspired by Edi Rama, the mayor of Albania's capital Tirana from 2003 to 2011, whose "Return to Identity" program had included the demolition of many of the city's small kiosks (not unlike the process in Tbilisi described in chapter 3) as well as painting old buildings in what locally came to be known as "Edi Rama colours" – bright violet, green, pink and yellow – in order to signify a break with the communist period in Albania.[14] But creating even further distance to the "grey" Soviet period, or the "shady" post-Soviet period, was not the only goal of Saakashvili's brush. A central aspect of the rapid reconstructions that had begun to take place throughout Georgia in the years following the revolution was also the need for Saakashvili and his government to make it clear to the population that things were in fact changing – that the revolution actually had real effects for everyone to see; that this was indeed a government of action.

As illustrated by the "George Bush stretch", the gentrification of the picturesque old town of Tbilisi, and the branding of Sighnaghi, this was not only a display aimed at local onlookers, there were other sets of eyes that were supposed to take notice as well: foreign investors, foreign tourists and foreign political and military allies. The country was in need of foreign goodwill and, not least, money. Constantly deteriorating relations with Russia had resulted in a Russian embargo of Georgian goods such as wine and mineral water, items that long had been central in terms of export. Reconstructions were costly, and although the government had been putting pressure on local businessmen to either sponsor or build something themselves, they still tore on the economy. And there were other posts on the state budget that needed to be covered too – not least that of military armament. Thus, as we will see, the pastel shade can be understood as a context for other kinds of facades, such as performances of patriotism and military capability.

Chapter 5

The Soldier

Parades

A loud sound of engines cuts through the air. Above us a formation of fighter jets appears, passes and disappears into the horizon. "These are our Georgian boys", Lola, a young woman in her twenties, says with a big smile on her face. For more than an hour, we have been watching what seems like an endless parade of uniformed soldiers from different divisions of the Georgian armed forces and reserve troops marching down Rustaveli Avenue displaying – apart from themselves – a selection of military hardware. It is May 26th 2006 and we are watching the military parade on Rustaveli Avenue that marks the Georgian Independence Day. Just as it was the case on May 26th in 2004 and 2005, the parade is said to be the largest-ever military parade in the history of Georgia.

Before the parade, President Saakashvili addressed the nation. He greeted "the strong, disciplined and combat capable Georgian army". A "new Georgia... which should be a source of pride for each Georgian", a "Georgia which will never bow head to enemy [and] which is capable of protecting its security and interests". Departing from this new militarily capable Georgia as a source of pride, Saakashvili continued his speech greeting youth, including members of the Patriotic Movement, the entire patriotic political spectrum, as well as Abkhaz and Ossetian "brothers and sisters" whom he predicted would soon celebrate Independence Day along with other citizens of Georgia. "God bless our homeland Georgia."[1] The symbolism was clear. Stressing that Georgia wanted nothing but peace; the parading soldiers were put forth as a sign of capability and patriotism. And, the nation was called upon to follow their lead in fighting for "freedom, liberty and success". Just as was the case with the myriad of reforms, painting and renovation projects described in the previous two chapters, the parades were not aimed solely at the local eyes. The military performance and the accompanying words from Saakashvili were sending a message to the Russian "big brother" that Georgia, through its close political alliance with Western powers and institutions, was building an impressive professional army capable of defending the country from Russian interventions and intrusions and, shortly, of returning the break-away territories of Abkhazia and South Ossetia. Georgia no longer had to "bow head" to any enemy. The parade and the marching soldiers were signs that Georgia could, and should, be a source of patriotic pride. And judging from the thousands of people who were cheering along Rustaveli Avenue that day a large share of the population seemed to agree. Lola definitely did.

May 26th does not mark the date of Georgian independence from the Soviet Union, which was declared by Zviad Gamsakhurdia on April 9th 1991. Rather, it marks the proclamation the Republic of Georgia in 1918 and, hence, independence from the Russian Empire. The short-lived period of Georgian independence between May 1918 and February 25th 1921, when the Red Army took Tbilisi and installed a Bolshevik government loyal to Moscow, was central to another event attended by the president on this particular day. Besides his speech at the military parade, he opened "the Museum of Soviet Occupation" – a new permanent exhibition at the National Museum in Tbilisi. The Museum is dedicated to the period of Soviet rule in Georgia between 1921 and 1991. Framing Soviet rule as occupation, something external and hostile to the Georgian nation, the exhibition explicates and evokes the repressive nature of the Soviet regime and depicts the resistance, and eventual victory, of the Georgian nationalist movement.

In the Museum of Soviet Occupation, Soviet soldiers and politicians were not Georgian but rather foreign intruders or national traitors. To some people, however, this logic was not as straightforward. Once again, it is time to leave Tbilisi for a while and enter a place that in several ways epitomizes the now and then ambivalent relationship between the image of the soldier and Georgian patriotism: the provincial town Gori where Katrine conducted fieldwork in 2010 and 2011.

Gori

If you pass Gori from the main highway, one of the first things you notice is a large complex of green buildings with Georgian flags waving in the breeze. If you take the second exit into town, the Tskhinvali Highway, the somewhat rough and bumpy road leads you right past the military complex on your right-hand side. The green buildings of the complex give a "clean" and almost neat impression. On your left, you see rows of identical small houses on little square plots of land, most of which – if it is the right season – will be covered with maize plants. Some of the small houses have had additions added onto them – some of brick, some wooden, some of sheet metal, and others of temporary constructions covered with tarpaulin. Small kiosks are placed next to each other on the roadside. Some offer petrol and wine in recycled plastic bottles, others cigarettes, vodka, candy and basic food stuff. The houses were built in 2008 to accommodate refugees from South Ossetia – just some 25 kilometres in the opposite direction. With its identical bungalows in strict lines, this refugee settlement (and others like it spreading over the hillsides on the outskirts of town) bears similarities with the military complex. In contrast with the military complex, however, which occupies an open and airy space, the bungalows give an impression of being almost claustrophobically cramped together, and neat is hardly the first word that springs to mind.

As you continue into town, you pass through the neighbourhood of Tsminda Tskhali: a patchy combination of Soviet-style five-storey apartment blocks, family houses, small kiosks and grocery shops, restaurants, and a shopping centre with large glass facades. In front of you Goris Tsikhe, a medieval fortress, lies on a hilltop surrounded by the coiled streets of the old town. Going right around the hilltop, you pass the central market and bus station. This is no doubt the busiest, noisiest and most hectic place in town, with bus and *marshutka* drivers calling out for passengers, market stands offering all kinds of things from building materials to flowers, pottery and food-stuffs, and old women offering juice, pastries, bananas, magazines and toys for the travelers both inside and outside the buses. Following the road left alongside the market, you reach Chavchavadzis Gamziri, the main shopping street in town with a myriad of small shops and second-hand outlets selling mobile phones, cameras, jewellery, clothing, study materials and kitchen utensils. Continuing along Chavchavadzis, you end up at the central square, Stalinis Moedani, spread out in front of the town hall. Looking to your left along the town's main thoroughfare, Stalinis Gamziri, you see the beginning of Stalin Park, leading to the Stalin Museum.

Gori is the administrative centre of the Shida Kartli region of central Georgia, located approximately 70 kilometres west of Tbilisi on the main highway crossing Georgia from east to west, close to South Ossetia. The green complexes dominating the view from the highway bear witness to the fact that the town was one of several locations to see the expansion of military infrastructure in the years following the revolution. In 2006, the Central Military Hospital was relocated from Tbilisi to Gori, and in January 2008, a NATO-standard base was established to accommodate the 1st Infantry Brigade of the Georgian ground forces. The names of the town's central square, main street and central park bear witness to another fact. Gori was the birthplace to Joseph Stalin.

War

Gori attracted particular international attention during the short-lived but intensive war between Russia and Georgia in August 2008, which was the culmination of years of tension and occasional violent clashes in the Russian-backed *de facto* independent republics of South Ossetia and Abkhazia. As we have mentioned in previous chapters, the waves of violent clashes in the two regions caused a great number of refugees and, consequently, internally displaced ethnic Georgians within Georgia proper. The last wave of refugees from South Ossetia, many of whom live in settlements such as the one passed on the road into town, has made these conflicts over territories highly visible in and around Gori.

The conflict over South Ossetia peaked in August 2008. Reacting to reporting of a Russian military build-up close to the northern border of the region, to clashes between Georgian and South Ossetian forces, and attacks on Georgian villages in the region, on August 7th the Georgian military launched an operation towards the South Ossetian capital, Tskhinvali, in order to "restore constitutional order".[2] According to Georgian intelligence, Russian troops had entered South Ossetia through the Roki Tunnel prior to the Georgian attack on Tskhinvali, which was thus framed as a response to a Russian assault on Georgian territorial integrity.[3] Fighting went on in South Ossetia for three days, with Russian forces reaching Tskhinvali on August 8th and supporting the South Ossetian side. On August 11th, Georgian ground troops were forced to retreat, and Russian forces began to advance into Georgia proper. Gori, situated approximately 25 kilometres from Tskhinvali, was the main staging area for the Georgian military during the battle.

On August 8th, Russian forces started bombing military targets in and around Gori. However, throughout the bombardment, which lasted for five days, several civilian locations, including apartment blocks and a school, were hit, and on August 12th a Russian cluster bomb hit the town's central square, killing and injuring a number of civilians. On August 10th, the Georgian Interior Ministry declared Gori unsafe, and a large number of civilians began to flee the town and its surrounding villages. Having been defeated in Tskhinvali, the Georgian army regrouped near Gori to try and prevent the Russians from taking the town. However, with reports of the Russian forces approaching Gori, Georgian troops were ordered to retreat in order to defend Tbilisi. In the afternoon of August 12th, the Georgian army began to abandon the town, as did the majority of the remaining civilians, and the next day Russian ground troops entered. The Georgian troops had suffered a rapid defeat. The Russian occupation of Gori lasted until August 22nd although some Georgian territories in the vicinity of Gori and the South Ossetian border remained under Russian control until October and some even to this day.

The problem of Stalin

Due to the Russian bombardment and occupation, Gori became a key symbolic site for framing the 2008 war not just as a disagreement over South Ossetia but as Russian aggression towards undisputed Georgian territory and the Georgian nation as such. This framing, however, was accompanied by certain predicaments.

It is a general stereotype in Georgia (and beyond) that the people of Gori love Stalin and that they are very proud of having a special link with one of the main political figures of the 20th century. When Katrine told Georgian friends such as Beka and Marina about her upcoming and ongoing research in Gori, the immediate reaction was most often a "why?" This would be followed by a remark, accompanied by an ambivalent giggle, that the residents of Gori were all loyal Stalinists. In 2008 Stalin was not only visible in terms of him giving name to a variety of public spaces. A six-metre-high bronze monument in his image dominated the town's central square. To some locals, in particular the elder generations, Stalin did indeed signify a time of order, strong leadership and military grandeur. Officially, however, the visual celebrations of Stalin had long been perceived as inappropriate: the monument was seen as an insult on the suffering of the Georgian nation during Soviet rule and the recent Russian occupation, and it was countering Georgia's efforts of aligning itself with the democratic West. Still, the authorities had been reluctant to remove the monument.

An interview with the then-Georgian Minister of Internal Affairs, Vano Merabishvili, in a Russian newspaper in spring 2010, illustrates the symbolic importance and rhetorical use of the Stalin Monument. In implicitly acknowledging that the government itself was hesitant to remove it, Merabishvili said that the Georgian authorities had tried to pay the Russian troops 50,000 USD to destroy the monument once and for all during the occupation of Gori. According to Merabishvili, however, the Russians refused because "they felt insulted. They were ready to take money for everything else, but not for that." Answering the Russian interviewer's question of whether he was implying that the Russians had Soviet values whereas the Georgians had European ones, Merabishvili answered:

> You said so. I will say otherwise. There are only two ways in the world – either to move towards western culture or to move nowhere. We have chosen the first one. And you? Has anything good happened in your country during these years? You have quarreled with your neighbors. They are afraid of you. You are afraid of each other. The society and police are in the state of war in your country. What have you built during past ten years? Therefore, you will never win the war with Georgia.[4]

A few days later, Merabishvili elaborated on his point in a

Georgian newspaper saying that:

> Russian officers were saying [...] 'Stalin is our ideal'... So, I was speaking about these attitudes – Russian officers and Russian army, who intruded into our land, are followers of Stalin, they are Stalinists.[5]

In short, the Russian soldiers' refusal to demolish the monument illustrated the fact, according to Merabishvili, that the Russians were employing Stalinist methods internally as well as towards their neighbours. And, because of this, they would remain stuck in the past, not moving anywhere, in contrast with Georgian aspirations. Within this framework, the Stalin Monument not only signified a certain reading of the past, but also the obstruction of a potential future as part of the "Western Culture".[6] In other words, the monument and the 2008 war were intricately connected. To the authorities, and many others, the Stalin Monument was an insult to the suffering of the Georgian nation in the past as well as to the people who lost their lives in the war. And, in summer 2010, the time had come. On June 24th to 25th 2010, the monument that had stood in front of the local town hall since the early 1950s was removed without warning in the dead of night.

The symbolic significance of Stalin was amply illustrated in a news briefing following the removal of the monument in which Saakashvili stated that the people "who led the Soviet invasion of Georgia" were not welcome in his country.[7] Then-Minister of Culture and Monument Protection, Nikoloz Rurua, echoed this view, stating that he believed that "Stalin was a political criminal, who led the Russian Bolshevik army into Georgia in 1921, [and] eventually carried out Georgia's occupation".[8] These statements reflected a particular interpretation and logic concerning the relationship between Stalin and the national past, present and future. In this interpretation, which also provided the subtext for the Museum of Soviet Occupation in Tbilisi mentioned earlier in this chapter, Stalin as a figure embodies equally the Bolshevik "occupation" of Georgia, the creation of the autonomous territories that continue to be out of reach, Soviet repression, and what was perceived as a continuation of this repression: Russian aggressions towards independent Georgia. The reasoning built heavily on a discursive equation between Stalin, the Soviet Union, and present day Russia. An equation in which Stalin embodies the suffering of the Georgian people, and the repressive and undemocratic political mentality of the Soviet era. Being an example of the kind of iconoclasm we described in the previous chapter, toppling the monument signified than Stalin was external to the Georgian nation and people and could not meaningfully be a source of local or national pride. Instead, the monument was to be replaced by a monument honouring the Georgians who fought in the 2008 war.

Alternative patriotism

It is a warm spring day of 2011. In a small square next to the Stalin Park in central Gori, elderly people dressed in old military uniforms with an abundance of medals are gathering with their families. In the corner of the square lies the War Museum, a small museum originally dedicated to Soviet participation in WWII. Today, however, beside the exhibition from Soviet times, the museum also hosts items and pictures connected with the conflicts in Abkhazia and South Ossetia, as well as the 2008 war with Russia. Behind the square is a wall monument to WWII depicting units of the Red Army carved in stone. In front of the wall is a row of memorial plaques with the names of local people who fell in WWII as well as in the conflicts in Abkhazia and South Ossetia in the 1990s. As people are gathering, young men are carrying in speakers, making sound tests and marking a provisional stage in the centre of the square. It is May 9th. The day that has since 1945 been celebrated as the day of victory of WWII in the Soviet Union and, after its collapse, most of its former republics.

The celebration, hosted by the local authorities, begins around noon, and the 100 or so people present gather in a half circle to watch and listen. The first event on stage is a young man emotionally reciting a poem devoted to the heroes of Georgia, while traditional Georgian polyphonic music plays in the background. When he is done, the then-Deputy Governor of Gori, Zurab Chkheidze, enters the stage:

> Hello, our dear veterans. Congratulations on this day. The day which Georgia has been celebrating and will always celebrate as it is the day of the victory over fascism. It is the day when fascism was defeated around the world. And the main role in this victory was played by Georgian brave men, and you, who are here now.[9] We will always mention these people. God bless you. We wish you a healthy life and many years. Many happy returns of this day!

Having thus welcomed the participants to the event, the celebration continues for another half an hour. The contributions on stage vary from the recitation of Georgian poems to children and youths singing Georgian pop songs and dancing traditional Georgian dances. The event seems detached from its origins. Images of Georgian nationality, culture and heroism are vividly invoked through traditional poetry, dancing and singing. But the historical context of the victory being celebrated is firmly left out of the event and the Soviet Union is not mentioned in any way – neither in positive nor negative terms. Paradoxically, it seems that a part of the past is being erased through the very process of commemorating it.

After the official event at the War Museum, a few hundred metres away, in front of Stalin's birthplace, an additional celebratory event is about to take place. As Katrine arrives, around 20 people are gathering outside the small cottage in front of the Stalin Museum. Some of them are carrying a painting of Stalin and a banner which reads: "I. V. Stalin's monument will be erected at the Museum". Among those present are the leader of the Gori branch of the Communist Party, Alexander, and the leader of the Stalin Society in Gori, Archil. We talk about the importance of today's celebrations, and the group's claim to have the Stalin Monument re-erected in front of the Museum. Archil explains: "It was announced that the Stalin Monument would be brought here, but now so much time has passed..." Alexander continues: "So everybody thinks that when they erect the monument, people will come from all over Georgia, and the government realize this", he says laughing. Archil continues: "It was a mistake for the government to take it down in the first place!"

As the participants gather to hear Alexander speak, it becomes evident that there is an element of protest to the event. Flanked by the banner and painting of Stalin, Alexander starts speaking through a megaphone:

> My dear friends. Congratulations on this Victory Day. Thank you very much for coming to our meeting. I would like to tell you that, unfortunately, our government likes to celebrate winning and the results of triumphs but does not consider who it was that brought about this victory. That's why it is the obligation of the Communist Party and Stalin Society, in spite of us being few here today, not to break with our tradition and to celebrate this day in front of the house of this great person [Joseph Stalin].

Most of the people attending this small event in front of Stalin's house had been present at the official celebrations next to the War Museum as well. It is evident from Alexander's speech, however, that this celebration was not sufficient, and did not appreciate the unique character of this particular victory. Rather, in his opinion, the official celebration had taken Victory Day hostage to forward government populist rhetoric of Georgian patriotism and triumph. In contrast, in this small gathering, victory was Soviet and highly connected with, and symbolized by, the figure of Stalin. Moreover, despite the general stereotype, such contrasts between government accounts of history and alternative readings were not exclusive to Gori.

A 2013 report from the Carnegie Endowment for International Peace shows that a number as high as 45 percent of Georgians carry some level of admiration towards Stalin. It is important to note, then, that a certain reverence for Stalin was by no means confined to Gori or to declared political opponents of the government such as the members of the local Communist Party above. This is not least because Stalin is still strongly connected with the victory over Nazi Germany in WWII – especially among the elder generation. He is considered a strong wartime leader, even if people may at the same time be critical of the political repressions and other aspects of his political reign. "For Georgians", the report concludes, "Stalin is much more a national icon than a political model".[10] Related to this is the fact that although many people among the elderly population in Georgia had experienced the Soviet Union, and a stronger, and for some very negative, presence of Stalin, they were still able to relate to this in very mundane ways – an example of this being when Emma laughingly recounted her Picasso-like rendition of Stalin in her childhood-classroom. For some, Stalin was simply someone who had been there, for good and bad.

When talking to people in Gori (and beyond) about Stalin's character the majority would distance themselves from the forced collectivization and famine of the twenties, the repression and terror of the thirties, the Gulag etc. But often these talks would be accompanied by additional reflections. Some would compare Stalin to Davit the Builder and Queen Tamar – both strong rulers of the Kingdom of Georgia in the "Golden Age" of the 11th to 13th centuries. They had also killed political enemies and built the nation using ruthless methods, but today everyone knows that such were the times, and they are both praised as Orthodox Saints. Saakashvili, as we mentioned earlier, gave his inaugural speech on the tomb of Davit the Builder in Kutaisi drawing exactly on this imagery of a strong national unifier and saviour. Similarly, a discussion of the hardships of the Orthodox Church during Soviet times and its revival after independence could often end with a comment that Stalin had been a great believer. As a child, people would remind Katrine, Stalin dreamt of becoming an Orthodox priest. He was singing in a local church choir and showed a remarkable talent for the special Georgian polyphonic songs. And, as a young man, his romantic poetic writings were acknowledged and published by Ilia Chavchavadze – perceived to be one of the nation's founding fathers. In other settings and situations, Orthodox Christianity, the polyphonic hymns, Chavchavadze and Georgian language poetry are all repeatedly and proudly invoked as symbols of the specific features of Georgian national identity – something that was evident in the official Victory Day celebrations. Paradoxical as it may seem, then, to a significant number of Georgians, Stalin as a figure seemed to embody not only the Soviet political regime he had led, but also national and local pride. He, a Georgian, displaying key Georgian virtues, had after all been one of the most significant political figures of the 20th century and played an important part in defeating Nazi Germany. Hence, through a particular lens, Stalin could just as well fit the ideal of a patriotic national soldier as that of a historical enemy to the Georgian people.[11]

Coda: Performance and ambivalence

In 2009, the year following the war with Russia, there was no Military Parade in Tbilisi to mark Independence Day. Already in

May 2008, the opposition, calling for Saakashvili's resignation on allegations of electoral fraud in the January 2008 presidential elections, had protested the Military Parade as an example of the violence nurtured by the government. In May 2009, the opposition who had been rallying on Rustaveli Avenue for more than a month announced a large-scale public parade on Independence Day and declared that they would physically obstruct the Military Parade if necessary. On May 13th Tbilisi mayor, Gigi Ugulava, announced that there would be no Military Parade that year, stating that the Parade was not a goal in itself and that the authorities would not give in to opposition provocations.

What was not mentioned as a reason in the briefing, but nevertheless could have contributed to the decision, was the situation in the army. On May 5th a commander of the Mukhrovani tank battalion had announced disobedience, mentioning the inappropriateness of the upcoming Parade as one of his reasons. In a televised address, Saakashvili explicitly connected the mutiny to a Russian plot to provoke tension and unrest – one in which they would never succeed, he assured. The incident resulted in a lengthy trial in which the key figures, who denied the charges, were sentenced for conspiracy and attempts to violently overthrow the government.

In May 2010, however, the tradition was resumed – even if the number of participating soldiers was smaller than in earlier parades. In his speech, Saakashvili poetically made an effort to rehabilitate the image of a patriotic and victorious Georgian army occupying a moral high ground; an image that had suffered under the defeat in 2008 and the increasing criticism of the government's rhetoric and priorities. "Listen to the sound of marching Georgian army and military hardware", he said when launching the parade. "This is not the sound of saber rattling, my friends; this is the sound of heartbeat of the Georgian statehood. No matter how hard the enemy tries to stop this heartbeat, it will never manage to do it."[12] It was clear that, by now, the enemy referred to was not only external to the Georgian state but also included the critics and opposition leaders who had obstructed the parade in 2009.

This inevitably led to a series of pertinent questions: Who was really to blame for the war? To what extent could anything come nearly close to a clear-cut answer to such a question? What in this whole scenario was reality and what was merely performance? Senses of ambivalence had long attached themselves to Saakashvili's leadership, and the revolutionary ideals in general. Such senses of ambivalence are not surprising seen in the context of revolutionary change in the region in general, Gerald Creed's depiction of ambivalence and disappointment towards post-revolutionary reforms in Bulgaria in the 1990s being a case in point.[13] In the context of post-revolutionary Georgia it is worth considering the perceptions of Marina not being sure whether Misha was really her president; Beka's decreasing enthusiasm as a result of the ongoing reconstruction projects; Gia's mistrust in whether the government would actually be able to solve social problems or whether it would naturally be external actors in the shape of NGOs taking care of this. But those kinds of ambivalence towards the political leadership were minor in comparison to those that erupted in the aftermath of the war.

Whereas there had been critics of the government's prioritization of military armament and (what was claimed to be) anti-Russian rhetoric before the 2008 war, the war had painfully demonstrated the consequences of Saakashvili's version of patriotic politics. Similar to the critique pointing to the pastel brush and surface renovations as mere facades for continuous interior decay, the performance of military grandeur introducing this chapter had by now become available as symbol of a mismatch between political representation and reality. For an increasing number of people, large-scale military parades showing off the army were just as much a reminder of defeat and continuous dependency on foreign powers as a source of national pride. For some people, Stalin, signifying a victorious war, provided an alternative source for a feeling of national power and grandeur. For others – in opposition and government circles alike – defeats and unfulfilled national aspirations were ascribed to plots of conspiring enemies of the nation. Enemies from the outside as well as within. An atmosphere of persistent dangers and threats had taken hold.

Chapter 6

The Mermaid

Big news

By the Black Sea coast a very different kind of threat is looming in the waters. In late October 2008 a mermaid is found on a beach south of Batumi, near the small settlement Gonio. It is not a mermaid in the form often depicted in fairy tales or myths: a beautiful creature half-fish half-woman. It is more of a monstrosity. It has human features but they are thwarted. This is not the figure of a Hans Christian Andersen story. This is something much more nightmarish and, strangely, real. Whether the creature was in fact truly real or not was the source of much discussion among residents of Batumi, where Martin is conducting fieldwork at this time.

"Have you heard the big news?" Nana asks him, "They found a mermaid in Gonio!" "A mermaid?!" "Yes! A two-metre-long fish with breasts and a head! I've got a film clip of it on my cell phone. Now I don't know whether I'll ever dare to swim again!" "I hadn't even heard anything about that." "It's been on Adjara TV." "I should probably buy a newspaper then." "It was a week ago but people are still talking about it. It's white." "Do you still have the clip on your phone?" "No, I deleted it – it was too scary, especially the sound it makes!" "Perhaps I can find it online then." "You definitely can. There must be more than one, it will also have a mother and a father!" "Maybe it will become a tourist attraction." "I don't think so, not when it's that big. At first I didn't believe it, but a lot of people have seen it. They wanted to send it to Tbilisi to be examined, but I think it's back in the sea again."

Nana is a psychologist and director of a local NGO assisting people with mental problems. She and Martin know each other through mutual friends at the NGO in Tbilisi where he conducted fieldwork two years earlier, and they now meet to drink coffee together once a week. But on this particular day coffee is completely overlooked. "Just a few months ago we were invaded by Russia and now there are killer-mermaids on our shores. Perhaps it is not so strange that such a monster appears right now", Nana says.

On his way home Martin passes by Nini's office. She's an office clerk and works right around the corner from his apartment. They had accidentally met during the early days of the war, and Martin had afterwards been watching TV with her and her family in the evenings to follow the developments. At that time, many locals had feared that the Russians would bomb Batumi through air raids, given that a military complex was located just outside the city, and because of the strategic importance of the port. Now Nini and Martin get together once in a while to chat. He asks her if she heard about the mermaid. "About what?" she says with a suspicious tone of voice. "About the mermaid, the one they found in Gonio." "I haven't heard anything about that." She opens a window towards the street and calls out to a woman selling newspapers outside; "Is there anything in the papers about a mermaid?" "No", the woman yells back. Newspapers are still almost solely covering the recent invasion. "Where did you hear about this?" Nini asks Martin. "One of my friends just told me, it was on Adjara TV", he says. "It's been on TV!" she yells to a couple of other women sitting in the front office who have been following their conversation. They confirm having seen it – "It's a terrible monster, a terrible time", they say. With autumn and winter storms soon arriving, along with heavy rainfalls that will most likely be flooding the street, it is not difficult to imagine that such mermaids would be able to swim all the way into the city centre. Chatter on the street continues as Martin leaves Nini's office.

The most surprising thing to emerge during initial conversations with local acquaintances about the mermaid was that, despite being described as monstrous or as a killer-mermaid, it was often depicted as an almost normal and even expectable occurrence in the aftermath of the war. Only a few months earlier, Martin had been walking around with Nana in darkened streets listening out for the possible sounds of Russian military aircrafts, and during dinners with Nini she had consequently been wearing heavy make-up as she "at least wanted to look good" should she be killed by a bomb. As Poti, a port city on the coast north from Batumi, was bombed, most people believed that Batumi would be next.

Paradise lost. Paradise regained. Paradise lost

Batumi had, during this same period, undergone massive reconstruction projects initiated by the government in an effort to re-establish the city as a central tourist hub by the Black Sea – it had become a prominent part of the government reconstruction projects mentioned in Chapter 4. And in many ways it was not surprising that this was so.

The train from Tbilisi to Gori continues towards the coast through the hills and forests of western Georgia. During the peak of summer one needs to reserve a seat well in advance, the train is packed with people seeking refuge by the coast from the heat in Tbilisi. The trip takes most of the day and along the way vendors stand ready at all stops to sell food through the window, and a large number of the passengers scurry out to manage three drags of a cigarette before the train moves on. At some point the landscapes flattens out, turning more and more into marshland, and vegetation changes along with it. As palm trees begin to appear, so do glimpses of the sea. The bay in which Batumi is located is breath-taking; green slopes gently glide down towards turquoise waters and the subtropical climate and warm winds lure residents from across the country towards the shores during summer. It was a multicultural city in Soviet times, visited and increasingly inhabited by people from other Soviet republics, many of whom were sent there as a reward upon their retirement, and besides becoming a residential and educational centre for sailors, the subtropical climate meant that the city steadily grew into a favoured tourist destination. Yet with the fall of the Soviet Union, tourism in Batumi had been greatly challenged. Tourists from the former Soviet republics now had the opportunity to go elsewhere, the escalating civil wars within Georgia throughout the nineties meant that few tourists from outside the former Soviet Union ventured there, and the increasingly strained relationship between the leadership in the Autonomous Republic of Adjara and the central government in Tbilisi entailed a decrease in tourists from Georgia proper. Tourist infrastructure fell into decay.[1]

The Adjara region itself had, in the months just after Saakashvili's inauguration, been one of the primary symbols of the success of the revolution. For over a decade it had been almost completely autonomous under the rule of former semi-despotic leader Aslan Abashidze. Outsiders had looked upon the region as a black hole on the peripheries of Europe – no longer a hotspot for tourism but for the illegal trade and trafficking of drugs, weapons and women. On our first visit to Georgia back in 2004 we had spent our final days in the country in Batumi, staying at Hotel Sputnik, an old Soviet-style hotel overlooking the city. There were not as such many hotels open in the city at this time, but as the region had not been under the control of the central government in Tbilisi throughout the 1990s there were no IDPs taking up residence in local hotels. Still, the hotel was largely empty of guests. It had only been a few months since Abashidze was ousted, and tensions were often highly visible. During one evening, while having dinner at the hotel, a group of determined local young men entered the restaurant and started a fight with another group of young men who were sitting at a table close to ours. Understanding little of what was going on, we grabbed our drinks and jumped into a large plant decoration while our table and chairs were toppled over by the fighting men. And as we left Georgia we did so by catching a ride at the border to Turkey with a marshutka also hosting a small group of prostitutes who were being driven to Trabzon – a sign that the trafficking of women had not altogether dissolved with the exit of Abashidze.

Despite the presence of a shadowy economy in Adjara, the region had, unlike the other two autonomous republics, South Ossetia and Abkhazia, steered clear of civil wars, and Abashidze and his closest family and allies had run the region as a small fiefdom. As the rise of Saakashvili saw the fall of Abashidze, who fled to Moscow, and Adjara once again came under the direct control of Tbilisi, reconstructions began in the city. Batumi was to become the Barcelona of the Black Sea – millions of Western tourists were to be attracted to these shores. The problem with Adjara, however, was that Adjara was not Abkhazia; although the shores and beaches running along Adjara's coastline had been visited by numerous tourists during Soviet times, it was the shores of Abkhazia further north that had been favoured. Whether it was Nina and Beka, Marina and Emma, local Tbilisi NGO workers, or Gia, Vanya and their friends who were reminiscing about past holidays at the seaside, they would all talk about the sandy beaches of Abkhazia and the beauty of its capital Sukhumi. But regardless of this, the return of Adjara to Georgia proper was a major success for Saakashvili's government, and until the sandy beaches of Abkhazia once again became Georgian soil, the stony beaches of Adjara could make do, and plans to renovate – or "Sighnaghify" – vast parts of the city while also initiating a series of new constructions, had begun. By the summer of 2008 the visitors present were mainly Georgians and Armenians. There were far from the millions hoped for by the president, but there were at least some. Yet the budding tourist industry was devastated by the war – tourists fled and nobody knew whether they would ever return. The railroad from Tbilisi to Batumi was temporarily blocked by the Russians, which meant that neither goods nor people reached the shore. And even if tourists were to return, who would ever dare enter the water if they knew a killer-mermaid was now lurking in the waves?

A ridiculed mermaid expedition

After Martin's conversations with Nana and Nini all plans for the rest of his day are put on standby. There is nothing else to do: he decides that he has to somehow get hold of the video clip of the mermaid so he can see it with his own eyes. Luckily his neighbourhood has electricity this time of day and he also manages to get his otherwise temperamental internet connection to work. It takes a few searches, but through Adjara TV's website he finally finds the clip. And the mermaid truly is monstrous. Forget about the Disneyfied version of Hans Christian Andersen's *Little Mermaid*. Forget anything about fairy tales and female grace capable of luring sailors into the depths of the sea. The video reveals a creature lying on its back in a bed in a small room. Most of all it looks like some sort of a stingray with markings of hands down its sides, a twisted but human-like face, and a long pointy tale. The camera filming the creature is shaking. There are two or three people in the room, mumbling unintelligibly to each other in Georgian. The mermaid is white and greyish and although it is difficult to see whether it is alive or not it appears to send out some sort a high frequency sound. Martin is not sure what exactly he had expected to see, but certainly not this. He does his best to maintain a degree of scepticism towards its authenticity, but still: monstrous or not, imagine if it was not a fake? Imagine if one could see this mermaid in real life? The idea rummages in his head all day. In the evening he is meeting up with one of the brotherhoods of young men whom he is conducting fieldwork among. For a long time they have been talking about how it would be nice to leave the city for a few days and go for a picnic at one of the beaches along the coast, collect clams below one of the old piers and barbeque them on the shore. Martin sees the possibility of a mermaid expedition.

While they are all playing cards in the evening Martin casually asks the guys whether they have heard the news about the mermaid. They have. New cards are dealt and stakes are settled. Nobody comments any further on it. They continue playing for a while. Martin suggest that perhaps they could all go to the Gonio in the weekend, have a barbeque on the beach, and – since it appears that it has been put back in the ocean somewhere around this area – maybe look for the mermaid. Smiles and scattered laughter can be seen and heard around the table. Emil, one of the young men, looks at Martin. "Do you remember that time when you asked me what distinguishes us from our parents?" he asks. Yes, Martin says. In fact, one of things he had been interested in during this particular fieldwork was how young people who had come of age after the dissolution of the Soviet Union differed from their parents. Emil had, last time he and Martin had been discussing this particular subject, noted that Martin could simply enter any of the numerous small casinos or "poker-shops" that had mushroomed in the city throughout the 1990s. "Our fathers are in there using their last coins. As if they believe in fairy tales and that they can become very rich very fast", Emil had said. The mermaid, he now noted, was merely another example of the exact same thing. Of a generation ready to believe in any illusion, a generation taking all rumours as reality. They themselves were perhaps in some ways a lost generation, but at least they were not superstitious.

Café del Bungalow

Martin meets with Emil one of the following days in the city centre. "Everywhere else things are different than here", Emil says, "young people are different". He was up late again last night, and now all he feels like doing is going the beach to swim and sleep. "I have nothing else to do than going out at night. Otherwise I just sit at home, and what can I do there? Eat, sleep." Martin asks him if he's tired. "Not in my head, but", he touches his chest, "in my soul". Emil has been working in one of the pop-up cafés that emerge in vast numbers along the city beach during summer. Most of them have already disappeared again as a consequence of the war and the one in which Emil is working will soon do the same. "What are you going to do when the café closes down?" Martin asks. "I don't know… I don't know", Emil says, "maybe work somewhere else, go somewhere else, I don't know".

They decide to go to the Botanical Gardens together, located a few miles further up the coast. As usual, Emil asks Martin to wear a cap before going to the small ticket window in front of the entrance. Locals can enter for free but foreigners have to pay a small amount for a ticket. Emil is afraid that Martin's blond hair will make the lady behind the glass suspicious of his origin, and there is no point in spending extra money when it can be avoided. Once inside, both as locals, they meet one of the janitors. He tells them that during Soviet times there were up to 300,000 visitors in the garden each year. Now it has been a good year if 3000 come. Much of the infrastructure in the garden is derelict, including the cable car that used to run through the entire premises. They go swimming at the beach below the garden. The water is clearer here than in the city, Emil notes, as they are further away from the oil harbour. After a few hours they take a minibus back to Batumi. As they move along the coastline they pass numerous small bars and cafés built in concrete and covered in colourful paint, remnants of the late 1980s. "Look", says Emil while pointing at them, "*Café del Bungalow*! We don't have Café del Mar here like they do in Europe, all we have is Café del Bungalow." As soon as the season stops, he continues, this is all there will be left. There will be no signs of the new pop-up cafés, they will all be packed away until next year, but the old bungalow ruins that are never in use will still be visible.

Not long after, the café where Emil has been working is also dismantled. It's a windy and grey day, and the other remaining cafés are being closed down as well. The music that has been constantly intermingling between cafés and bars during the summer season is now gone, chairs are being stacked and bottles removed. As the sun goes down all lights are turned off. The beach is empty. Emil puts the remaining bottles in a bag and carries them to a van that it waiting close by. The other people who have been working in the café are sitting on the floor in silence, chain-smoking and yawning. The ashtrays are gone, so they use the floor. Storms are becoming frequent on the horizon, and this evening there is lightning over the sea. Parts of the city seems to have disappeared and *dys*-appeared at the very same time. That is, the image of the city as a reinvigorated tourist site has gone missing, while that which this image was supposed to have supplanted is unintentionally foregrounded. The new tourist infrastructures are left as hollow shells that have had their contents and meanings torn out of them. Rather than pointing towards a future of ever-growing tourism, they suddenly come to stand side by side with the abandoned and empty tourist infrastructures of the Soviet period.

Illusion and monstrosity

The lack of pay-off from the opening towards the West had caused widespread disillusion in Georgia since 1991. Many had turned to religion or magic as a means to uphold the dream of a better future. But this kind of search for the re-enchantment of an otherwise disillusioned everyday life was surprisingly absent among the young men in Batumi whom Martin had come to know. It was not that disillusionment was not part of their daily lives. Only a few of them had an education and ever fewer had a job. They lived on a day-to-day basis and some were engaged in various kinds of crime.

In many ways, the young men were the misfits of Batumi. Like many of their age-mates in Tbilisi they would spend most of their time engaging in birzha, hanging on street corners and walking aimlessly around the city centre. This had to be done with some caution though, as local police had begun to strike down on such behaviour, trying to make sure that the street, at least during summer, looked proper and safe. Emil and his friends had on several occasions been stopped by the police at random and taken to the station in order to give urine samples that tested them for drugs. Imprisonment was a possibility if a test proved positive, and prisons were known hellholes that everyone should avoid. So measures had to be taken to not be picked up on suspicion of being on or selling drugs, even though that was exactly what was going on. Emil therefore taught Martin how to walk at a proper pace, how to always be clean-shaved, and how to always wear as proper clothes as one has, all of this to minimize potential suspicion.

But although life for Emil and his friends was without any immediate prospects, they didn't channel their hopes and dreams for the future into activities such gambling or magic, nor their disillusionment towards the present into a belief in a monstrous mermaid. It was, they insisted, exactly this that distinguished them from their parents. No matter whether it concerned the state, the church, casinos or mermaids, they expressed a high degree of scepticism towards the world around them. Sure, the war against Russia had been a terrible event, but for them this did not provide a context for seeing mermaids as suddenly being a part of reality.

So Martin never managed to go mermaid-hunting. Yet the appearance of the mermaid (real or not) outlined some of the ways in which illusion, disillusion and scepticism were expressed and experienced differently among different groups in the city. For some, such as the psychologist Nana, the monstrosity of the mermaid was not as such surprising, because it had appeared in the aftermath of another kind of monstrosity – the Russian invasion and the instability of society in general. The mermaid was but yet another sign of a world gone mad. For others, such as the young men in the brotherhoods, rumours of the mermaid were also not as such surprising in the sense that they were illustrative of the kind of illusions that their parents' generation was prone to believe in but that they themselves were highly sceptical towards. This did not mean that they felt less lost but that they at least saw themselves as being more realistic or pragmatic in the way they handled their sense of disillusionment.

The same pragmatism was evident in their relation to politics. After the war the opposition toured the country and held rallies against the government in a series of major cities. In order to secure a crowd at these events, groups of people, most often young men, would be brought along. At the local office of one opposition party in Batumi it was possible to sign up to go, sometimes being paid or sometimes just getting a free ride to another city. Emil and Martin go to this office at one point, as Emil would like to take a trip to Tbilisi. He doesn't have the money for a train ticket so taking an opposition-rally marshutka for free is a good alternative option. "I don't really care about politics at all", he tells Martin, "and I don't think I'll actually stay at the rally unless I find some of my friends there. I'll just spend the day and night in Tbilisi and then jump on the marshutka when it heads back here." He also confides that he has rarely voted – if he did it would either be based on a random choice or done as a favour to a relative or neighbour who supported this or that political party. Like with most of his friends, Emil was not sceptical towards particular politicians or politics but rather towards politics in general. As with the mermaid, politics was just a charade.

Coda: Disenchantment and scepticism

The monstrous has a tendency to appear in relation to societal instability, as Maria Louw has shown in her description of the appearance of a serial killer in Kyrgyzstan,[2] as has the appearance of illusion. The turn to magic and gambling was a widespread phenomenon in many former Soviet Republics during the 1990s.[3] The fascination with quick wealth through pyramid schemes, and engagements with occult practices and money magic, were however not confined to the post-Soviet space; they became widespread phenomena across the globe around the turn of the millennium.[4] Yet such practices seemed to have a heightened salience in many post-Soviet contexts where disappointment about the lack of financial gains of capitalism led many to seek out alternative forms of gaining wealth or alternative forms of belief.

Search of enchantment in a world of disillusionment, however, was not immediately to be found among the young men in Batumi whom Martin was conducting fieldwork among. It was not that there were no possibilities of letting luck play a role in one's life for residents in the Batumi. As mentioned, particularly in the old part of the city, poker-shops and small casinos were numerous – on every street there was one to be found. Tucked in-between these one could find a *lombardi* – a pawnshop – where items of various sorts could be exchanged for a small amount of money. Many of the young men frequently visited a *lombardi* but it was not to secure a few lari for gambling. For some it was in order to get money to buy credit for their cell phones and for others it was to save money to help out a friend in trouble.

It might, of course, very well be that the video clip of the killer-mermaid was merely a construction; that it was just some kind of doll that somebody had made for fun. But in some ways this doesn't really matter. The appearance of monstrosity in Batumi generated its own realities and stories; even though the mermaid might have been purely fiction, stories about it were each grounded in their own realities. The monstrous, in this sense, has its own social life, which cannot just be disregarded.[5]

On the one hand its appearance came to reflect Nana and Nini's insecurities about whether making Batumi a centre for tourism would at all be feasible. One the other hand it reflected how the disillusionment experienced by the young men had resulted in a much more general or extreme kind of scepticism and experience of doubt, directed towards the state, the church, casinos, politics and mermaids alike.

So while the Adjara region was an image of success for Saakashvili and his government, it was not an uncontested one. There may have been differences in the way people related to the authenticity of the killer-mermaid, but whether believing it real or not, people related it to their scepticism towards the government. "Sighnaghization" had set in, but would that really matter?

Chapter 7

The Hoax

Headlines

Eight pm, Saturday, March 13th 2010. *Kronika,* a news broadcast on the TV channel Imedi, opens with the anchor announcing that the president is about to make a special statement on the current situation in Georgia.[1] With a caption reading "Mobilization of the occupying forces; Akhalgori-based military unit on combat readiness", the host of the program informs us that there have been reports that the Russian forces in South Ossetia have declared to be ready for combat and that it cannot be ruled out that they will march towards Tbilisi. As he continues telling about how this news has caused panic in Gori, Tbilisi and other Georgian cities, we see startling footage showing traffic jams caused by people fleeing, queues at gas stations, and hectic chaos in the streets.

The next story of today's news reports how a number of people have been wounded during unrest in Tbilisi with nine of them still remaining in the hospital. As the image switches to footage of people fighting and arguing with police officers and thousands of people protesting in the streets, we are told that "the unrest in Tbilisi started on June 7 after unknown persons opened fire on protesters gathered in the centre to protest against the election results". The two opposition leaders Nino Burjanadze, who is a former parliamentary speaker, and Zurab Nogaideli, who is a former prime minister, both of whom have recently met with Russian prime minister Putin, are mentioned as being key organizers of the protests. Once again the image switches, and as we see footage from a joint meeting of the opposition leaders, we are informed that the opposition has made a joint statement declaring the government illegal and announcing their establishment of a People's Government of Georgia that will free the country from the dictatorship and tyranny of Saakashvili. The news report continues with a story from breakaway South Ossetia where there has been a "life attempt" on Eduard Kokoity, the leader of the self-proclaimed country. Burjanadze and Nogaideli have arrived in Tskhinvali and have in a statement echoed the Russian authorities in blaming the Georgian government for plotting the attack on Kokoity.

As elsewhere in the country at this moment, the living room at the Nutsubidzes' in Gori is buzzing. The family and a couple of their friends, who had the TV running in the background while gathered around the table for a small improvised supra as so often on Saturdays, get increasingly baffled and disturbed. All of a sudden, all eyes and ears are directed towards the TV set. What is going on? Is the country sliding into chaos? Is this yet another revolution?

Russian intervention

A while into the program, the anchor, looking very nervous and juggling his papers, reveals that a little while ago they have received information that the Russian army is mobilizing for battle in parts of Armenia and the North Caucasus and are ready to cross into Georgia and to use new Russian weaponry. Meanwhile, he continues, we can also let you know that the Georgian army is mobilized and that fortifications of Tbilisi are taking place while the Georgian army is being gathered from different parts with heavy artillery around the capital. The Ministry of Defence is making no comments as of now. The news speaker touches his earpiece and listens attentively for a while. Then he announces that they are in possession of a statement from the Russian president that has been aired by Russian TV. The caption shifts to "Russian intervention", and President Medvedev appears on the screen sitting in an armchair in a study and gives his statement dubbed with a Georgian voiceover:

> Based on the developing news, Russia is obliged to make final decisions in order to maintain peace and harmony between the countries in the Caucasus. We can say that based on the wishes of the people, including hundreds of thousands of Russians there, the Georgian people, Ossetians and Abkhazians all want peace. At this moment, only one thing stands in the way of peace: Saakashvili. He is doing everything he can to maintain the region in a state of destruction and chaos. He is a terrorist representing an imminent threat to the people and the Caucasus region. Russia wants peace and good relations with all countries of the Caucasus, especially Georgia. We can't let centuries of brotherly relations be hampered by Saakashvili. So, right now, military operations have begun to free Georgia from the tyranny of Saakashvili and for the maintenance of everlasting peace in the region. We are not going to battle the Georgian people or their army. The less resistance we meet, the faster liberation will take place along with peace for our repressed neighbouring country's people.

The news speaker reappears on the screen and reminds us that this was Medvedev making a statement on the decision to intervene in Georgia. He has just been notified, he continues, that all government buildings and the president's administration are being evacuated, and that Saakashvili is in Tbilisi – although his whereabouts are being kept secret. Right now in Armenia, he carries on, the Russian forces have officially crossed the border and are headed towards Tbilisi, and also from Akhal Gori, Russian tanks are on the move. The anchor's speech is accompanied by footage of tanks rambling down a dusty road and a fighter jet breaking a bright sky.

With a Georgian voiceover, we receive filmed statements from different Russian politicians and people on the streets. Several comments point to Saakashvili's mistake of trying to side-line Russia in his eagerness to cooperate with the US and NATO, and argue for the reasonability of Medvedev's decision to finally restore the brotherly relations with Georgians. However, we also see Russian opposition figures denouncing the ongoing invasion, calling for international sanctions, and praising the bravery of the Georgians trying to get out of the imperialistic claws of Moscow and choosing democracy.

Once again we return to the studio. The anchor announces that he has received more breaking news. Apparently, according to a spokesperson of the "People's Government of Georgia", three battalions previously on their way to defend Tbilisi have decided not to support Saakashvili's criminal regime. Instead, declaring their allegiance to the People's Government, they turned around on their way towards Gori from where they will fight for the liberation of Georgia from Saakashvili. Showing footage of the central square in Gori and Burjanadze, smilingly greeting military personnel, we are told that the People's Government went to Gori and met with the deflected battalion to congratulate them on their patriotic decision. Speaking from Gori, Burjanadze has encouraged all military personnel to do the same, since, according to her and the People's Government, Saakashvili is a criminal clinging to power while destroying the country.

The next feature shows President Barack Obama giving a live statement from Washington in which he urges Russia to stop her military campaign against Georgia. Fading out of the footage of Obama in front of the White House, the anchor announces that right now Secretary of State Hilary Clinton is on her way to Moscow to mediate. Shortly after, accompanied by video of fighter jets throwing bombs from a clear sky, we are informed that a few minutes ago, Russia conducted air strikes on Tbilisi airport and on the Senaki and Gori military bases. And then, breaking, sensational, yet unconfirmed, news: President

Saakashvili has allegedly been assassinated and violent clashes are currently taking place in Mtskheta, just outside Tbilisi...

Half an hour has passed and a jingle signals that the news program is over.

A simulation of realistic plots

The news report was a fake. As it ends we return to the studio where a Special Report program continues. The female anchor in the studio begins by addressing her audience: "for those who have just joined us, I want to say that these were not real chronicles of today. These were possible events that may take place in early June... *Kronika* has offered you to imagine what should not happen." Actually, the video of approaching tanks shown in the broadcast had mainly been real footage from the war with Russia in 2008 with mock voiceover. According to the TV station the purpose of the fake news report was to create an illustration of what could very likely happen again. Prior to airing the broadcast, the host in the studio had explained that what followed was only a simulation – a worst-case scenario – of what might happen in the future. However, this disclaimer was lost on all the people who tuned in on the show after the warning, such as the Nutsubidzes in Gori and many others who had followed the half-hour broadcast with increasing bewilderment and anxiety.

In hindsight, some elements of the report should probably have caused immediate suspicion about its veracity. First of all, the mentioning of the unrest in Tbilisi starting on June 7th after the local elections was an obvious clue that the program was actually reporting on events that had not yet taken place, given that it was aired in the month of March. Secondly, the revolutionary statement from a joint opposition that a "People's Government of Georgia" had been established, and Burjanadze and Nogaideli's alleged call for mutiny in the armed forces, were both given second-hand by a narrator rather than by voiced footage of the opposition leaders themselves. Lastly, the statements made from President Medvedev, President Obama and other foreign "contributors" to the broadcast were all provided with a Georgian voiceover blurring the actual speech and making it impossible to judge what was actually being said. On the other hand, this practice of providing statements made in foreign languages with a Georgian voiceover is common in real news broadcasts as well. In any case, these hints and the critical questioning they could have sparked were lost on a majority of the viewers. In effect, the 30-minute broadcast sparked panic and alarm all over the country. Mobile networks crashed, lines formed at the gas stations and some people got ready to flee their homes. It was even reported that the rate of heart attacks in the country had risen dramatically during and after the broadcast. For a while the actual scenario in the streets came to be a reflection of the simulation.

Once it was realized that the broadcast had been a hoax, fear turned to anger and people started to gather outside the TV studio to protest. The spokesperson of the President, Manana Manjgaladze, rushed to the station to tell them that they had made a big mistake. "The president sent me here to tell the television staff that when such a program is being made, despite the fact that our country is still being subjected to certain threats, there should not only be a verbal warning in advance, but also a special on-screen banner saying it is an imitation."

The following day Saakashvili himself repeated the criticism. However, he also made the point that people had panicked exactly because the TV program had shown a scenario that was very likely to happen if the Russians were to have their way. "I believe yesterday's report will become an obstacle to them fulfilling their plans, despite the nervous reaction", he said – thus suggesting that the episode had sparked reflection and awareness among the population of the dangers of opposing the government line and fraternizing with Russia. Politicians such as

Burjanadze and Nogaideli, who had met with Putin, were portrayed as prime examples of traitors and enemies of the Georgian people.

Members of the opposition were not alone in criticizing the program. The Patriarch, Ilia II, condemned the program as an abomination – an insult on the Georgian people and army. And in the days that followed, the US and British ambassadors to Georgia, as well as the European Monitoring Mission and other representatives of the international community, all expressed their concerns about the fake news report, pointing out that it was irresponsible and could very likely have destabilized an already fragile situation in the country. On March 15th, reflecting the statement made by Saakashvili the previous day, the president's spokesperson replied to the condemnations and concerns expressed by the international community, saying that:

> The Georgian government believes that instead of concentrating attention on violation of standards of ethics by a television station, the attention of the international community should be focused – as it is – on such real facts like Russia's occupation, ethnic cleansing, non-fulfilment of the ceasefire agreement, open actions by Russia directed to overthrow the democratically elected Georgian government, and attempts to restore so called spheres of influence.[2]

The TV broadcast in many ways mirrored a well-known narrative of Russian schemes and infiltrations. As we have seen in the previous two chapters, at this point in time, the Russians aiming to destabilize domestic Georgian politics and prevent the consolidation of national prosperity and international alliances was a well-established idiom. In that sense, Saakashvili's statements, and the TV broadcast as such, fed into a more general stream of accounts of Russian intentions, allegations against some opposition politicians for plotting with Russia to overthrow the government, and insinuations about the lack of patriotism of ordinary people critical of the government in general, and its rhetoric about Russia in particular.[3]

Government against the people

Several opposition parties, on the other hand, made statements condemning the fake report. The opposition leaders who had been portrayed as being Moscow's agents in the program were quick to ascribe the program to governmental propaganda. Burjanadze, who was portrayed as a founder and speaker for the "People's Government" in the program, but who had also been one of the main figures to stand with Saakashvili during the Rose Revolution, stated:

> I can't imagine any normal country where things like that could be possible. Where someone could call you a traitor or agent of another country without any response. And I am more than sure that the Georgian people will make a choice for stability, for unity of the country, for democracy, and for that, we need to change this criminal irresponsible government.

The allegations from the opposition and parts of the population that the government was behind the program were supported by the well-known alliance between the head of Imedi TV, Giorgi Arveladze, who was a former government member, and the president. Considering this close connection the program would, according to the opposition, logically have been made in agreement with the authorities, the argument went.

A few days after the airing of the fake report, a taped phone conversation appeared. The recording allegedly featured a conversation between the head of Imedi TV, Giorgi Arveladze, and his head of news and political programs, Eka Tsamalashvili, which strongly indicated that they had deliberately avoided clearly notifying the viewers that the news report was a hoax. In the phone conversation a man and a woman are discussing the broadcast of the fake report. The woman points out that the program seems to appear very realistic and that people who would tune in after the initial warning that it was a fake might well believe it to be true. To her suggestion that there should be a banner running all through the program indicating that the report was fiction, the man responded: "I was speaking to Misha yesterday and he asked me if it would be aired like a regular Kronika... I responded positively, but told that it would be said in advance that it's a simulation. But he told me not make an announcement in advance." The woman then warns the man that if they do not, as a minimum, warn viewers in advance, people might be scared. The conversation ends with the man saying "In the beginning of the broadcast do not explain in details that it's all fake".[4]

Arveladze's mentioning of Misha, the name by which Saakshvili is most often referred to among the public, added to the speculations that the president had been involved in, or had even ordered, the report. Publicly responding to the recordings, neither Arveladze nor Tsamalashvili denied that it was their voices on the tape. They did however both claim that the tape was a fabrication that consisted of bits and pieces of things they had said under different circumstances. A conversation as the one put forth in the recording at stake had never taken place, they insisted. In commenting on the recording, Arveladze said that this was just "another provocation with Russian special services obviously behind it. It was posted on a website with links to Russian special services."[5]

The claim from Arveladze and Tsamalashvili that their conversation had been fabricated made several opposition figures call for an independent investigation into the authenticity of the recording with the assistance of foreign experts. However, echoing Arveladze's allegation that the tape was fabricated by

FSB (the Russian Federal Security Service), the authorities refused to engage with the allegations stating that creating internal disunity in Georgia was exactly what the Russians were aiming at. Not surprisingly, these comments were received by opposition figures and critics as evidence that the authorities actually had been involved and, hence, did not want the truth to be established beyond doubt.

The shut-down of hope

It is noteworthy that the relationship between the Imedi Broadcasting Company and the government of Saakashvili had not always been friendly. Originally founded in 2001, Imedi had been the first independent broadcasting company to appear in independent Georgia. It had gained international attention in late 2007 during anti-government protests taking place in central Tbilisi, in which 50,000 to 100,000 people demonstrated against alleged corruption within the government. On November 7th the protests turned violent as police used teargas and water cannons against the crowd, and a state of emergency was declared that lasted until November 16th. Saakashvili held that the country was witnessing an attempted coup d'état and accused the Russian intelligence service of being involved.

During the protests in 2007, Imedi had been the only station that was officially critical towards Saakashvili, and afterwards it was forcibly seized by government troops. A running joke at the time was that the "the president has shut down hope" – "*imedi*" meaning hope in Georgian. But the take-over of Imedi also gained international attention and was condemned by Human Rights Watch, the UN and NATO – the latter's criticism posing somewhat of a problem for Saakashvili as he had long had a stated goal of Georgia joining NATO. The crisis of the anti-government protests was eventually solved through a compromise that pushed forward planned presidential elections to January 2008 – an election Saakashvili would go on to win with

53.7 percent of the votes. Imedi, however, effectively stayed under government control until 2012.

Coda: Simulation and conspiracy

Was the opposition plotting with Russia to overthrow the government in connection with the upcoming local elections? Were Saakashvili and Imedi deliberately deceiving and causing panic among ordinary people in order to hold on to power and privileges? Or, was the incriminating tape recording a fabrication by the Russian intelligence services?

As opposed to the mermaid in Batumi, which was inherently unnatural, the Imedi hoax struck another degree of reality. The report might have caused a nation-wide scandal, but even more so it demonstrated a general public fear and belief that the reported scenario was not at all unlikely. After all, even if the broadcast consisted of video clips detached from their original contexts, the footage portrayed events and episodes that had, in fact, really happened. And, even though much of it had been accompanied with a mock voice-over distorting the message, recent experience combined with prevailing political rhetoric contributed to it being taken at face value. In other words, the immediate popular reactions – panic and uproar – pointed to a more general atmosphere that had over the past years been produced and maintained through the imagining of persistent dangers to the Georgian nation as well as a concrete experience of daily life being determined by political plots and hidden agendas. In a sense, the simulation – deliberately or not – for a while produced in reality the fake scenario it had portrayed. Likewise, the subsequent allegations of the government plotting and deceiving the Georgian people, in order to manipulate public opinion prior to the local elections, also tapped into already-existing narratives and theories, and the statements made by opposition leaders in the wake of the report were actually very similar to the mocked statements in the report in terms of their wording.

The narrative plot of the fake news report, the panic it immediately sparked in the public as well as its political aftermath, were illustrative of an atmosphere of suspicion and conspiracy that had increasingly come to dominate political discourse as well as public characterizations of political events. Conspiracy theory here, should not be understood as illogical or paranoid, but rather as a response to a particular political reality and experience that had at this point in the post-Revolution years become prevalent. In a basic sense, we may see a conspriacy theory as an "explanation which postulates that an event is the (at least partly intended) effect of activities that have been secretly planned and carried out by several actors".[6] In this definition the Imedi hoax, and the subsequent allegations and explanations from government and opposition alike, was exemplary of conspiratorial politics. That is, of politicians being engaged equally in conspiration (plotting against opponents and adversaries) and conspiracy theorizing (conjuring up the presumed plots of others).

Hence, while the Revolution had initially been a call for democracy, transparency and the elimination of political corruption, the revolutionary project and the constant need to expose enemies plotting against its cause, had produced a political environment in which the distinction between theatrical simulation and reality was blurred, and in which sincerity and clarity were increasingly sought through reference to secrecy and opacity.

Chapter 8

The Theatre

Hospital openings

It is January 2012. Katrine and Marina sit in Marina's living room in Tbilisi drinking tea and watching the evening news. Saakashvili appears on screen enthusiastically speaking to a crowd of people gathered in front of a newly constructed building. "Ah, you see? Every day our Misha is opening a new hospital somewhere", Marina says. "It is something very interesting..." she adds – giggling as she often does when commenting on politics or the president. A giggling that we have both come to recognize as a sign of her pointing to a profound irony of events, or, as is often the case, life in general. "Look he is in your town, in Gori!" "Really?" Katrine says skeptically, "I'm surprised that so many people are there. I don't think I have ever seen so many *gorelebi* in the same place before." They laugh. Katrine is indirectly playing with the belief often jokingly expressed by Marina: that Gori must have been a horrible and boring place to live, where nothing ever happened. Katrine's skepticism on the other hand, draws on the fact that during her fieldwork in Gori in 2010 and 2011 she failed to get acquainted with much more than a handful of people who enthusiastically supported Saakashvili. Rather, opposition, critique and mockery had been the rule. Nevertheless, as the president gives his speech in front of the newly opened hospital with medical personnel dressed in white smocks, an excited audience is cheering and clapping.

Saakashvili talks about the present as an epoch of revival. Never since the golden ages of Davit the Builder and Queen Tamar has so much construction taken place. "Certain people" in the country, he says, might be trying to draw Georgia back into a dark past. But they will never succeed – Georgia is on a track moving forward, and there is no going back. The reason for this is that the developments are the result of a joined effort – not the work of a ruler alone:

> Every citizen of Georgia, no matter where he/she lives has the same opportunities… Georgia is moving forward and as long as we keep gradually building, making, and creating in the conditions of freedom nothing can stop our progress… Everyone knows that the government will do everything for people to come for treatment to these hospitals. If the government were only to care about its family members then a small clinic would be enough…[1]

The words are followed by more applause from the audience. As the president leaves, people are cheering: "Misha! Misha! Misha!"

A few days later Katrine is watching the evening news again – this time in the company of Pati, her former landlady in Gori. Once again a hospital is being opened. "I saw on the news a couple of days ago that Misha had opened a new hospital in Gori," she says. Pati nods and smiles. "I was surprised that so many people were there…" Katrine adds. "I was there too", Pati laughs. "Really?" Katrine asks doubtfully – knowing from numerous conversations and discussions that Pati and her family are anything but fans of the president. "They had lists with our names at the school, and we were told to go… and so we went", she explains matter-of-factly, before bursting into yet another cunning giggle.

Marina and Pati both seem to find the hospital openings ironic and somewhat amusing. But what was it that was apparently so amusing about the president appearing on the news on a daily basis opening another new provincial hospital?

One hundred hospitals

The story of the series of new hospitals being opened begins already in the mid-1990s when a range of local and international reports concluded that the country's hospital sector was simply too big in terms of infrastructure and resource capacity, and in 1999 the World Bank financed and developed a plan for restructuring the sector.[2] The main proposition in the plan was that one group of existing hospital facilities was to remain in the public domain, a second was to be privatized and a third to be sold as real estate. Following the revolution the new government agreed to concur with the plan, which at this time had begun its implementation. The new officials however wanted to elaborate on the plan by including guaranteed access to a comprehensive healthcare service within a 30-minute drive for the majority of the population. The previous plan, it was argued, had focused too explicitly on Tbilisi and neglected the provision of healthcare in more remote regions in the country.

Already by 2006, however, then-Minister of State Reforms, Kakha Bendukidze, announced a new plan, as he was frustrated with the results achieved so far. In order to speed up the process of guaranteed healthcare, Bendukidze proposed to remake healthcare services by privatizing all hospitals and healthcare facilities in the country which, in his interpretation, would lead to increased patient choice along with increased competition and thus ultimately to healthcare services of a higher quality. The plan was approved by the government in 2007 and consisted of 100 new hospitals being built by private investors within a period of three years. Investors were thus not to bid on running existing hospitals. Rather they were to build new hospitals on the territory of already-existing state-owned facilities. Written into the announced tenders, however, was a note stating that investors could convert the land and facilities for other uses after a seven-year period. Hence, if running a hospital or healthcare clinic for seven years did not prove rentable investors were in principle free to close it down and open a hotel on the premises instead.

Criteria for selecting investors were at first based on the quantity of hospitals and beds. But soon after the first tenders were announced an added criterion suddenly appeared: speed. The government wanted to ensure that results were achieved as soon as possible, even though the originally proposed frame of a three-year building period was not as such a long period of time, and had in fact been prolonged by insistence from the World Bank from two to three years. But this was not the only amendment to tenders appearing along the way. By the sixth and seventh tender announcements another addition was made. Under a sub-heading entitled "miscellaneous" it was mentioned that investors were responsible for the removal and resettlements of any IDP families living in the state-owned properties, without further information about how this should be done. Reflecting our points from Chapter 3 about the "disappearing" and "outsourcing" of social problems through a series of neoliberal reforms, the privatization of hospitals thus also came to include a privatization of parts of the IDP problem faced by the government.

An empty hospital

The Racha-Lechkhumi region is a province located in north-western Georgia. The terrain in the province is hilly and mountainous and, with the exemption of only a few relatively flat valleys, mechanical agriculture in the region has historically been difficult if not impossible to practice. In this way it contrasts with many other regions in the country by lacking large cash crops and agricultural markets. During the Soviet period small power stations were set up making possible a minor timber industry, as well as an arsenic mine and factory in the village Uravi, which provided some degree of local employment. Along with these, the harvesting of grapes was one of the only industries existing in the region. Since the dissolution of the Soviet Union there had been little production in the region; unlike other provinces of Georgia, there had been little official focus on the region as a potential tourist destination, and poor infrastructure in terms of deteriorated roads entailed that getting there and back was an arduous affair. This meant that national and international investments were comparatively low and job opportunities consequently equally so. In official statistics, the vast majority of the population in the region is represented as "self-employed" (out of 323 employed, 232 appear as "self-employed" in the 2010 statistic). This, however, covers everyone with access to a piece of land (even a garden), since one is then considered a farmer. In reality however such "farming" is rarely enough to secure a livelihood.

In the region at large, and particularly in the smaller villages, there had been a general tendency of depopulation with individuals and families moving to cities outside the region, mainly Tbilisi. The tendency was statistically higher here than in any other region and was naturally followed by a decrease in birth rates. Further, the deteriorated roads made it almost impossible to move to and from villages during winter, a period when many of these thus lay empty as families otherwise risked being trapped in their houses or villages for months at a time. Compared to other regions, Racha-Lechkhumi also had the lowest number of physicians (of all specialities), the lowest number of hospital units and hospital beds, the lowest number of paramedical personnel, and the lowest number of medical institutions rendering out-patient services.[3]

With this context, Racha-Lechkhumi was thus one of the regions that would ideally benefit greatly from the new hospital program. And, as tenders were announced, a new hospital was indeed constructed. The new facility was built by the insurance company "IC Group", and the hospital was opened by Saakashvili in 2011. Besides regular healthcare provisions, it was to include the principle of tele-medicine. That is, online consultations with specialists in either Tbilisi or abroad, a practice that was tested during the opening ceremony as Saakashvili himself talked to a Georgian doctor residing in Denmark.

By 2013, as Martin visited the hospital during fieldwork on regional development in Racha-Lechkhumi, one feature was striking in the new facility: it was largely empty. While some rooms or sections were simply not in use, others appeared to never have been fully completed, and some bore traces of slowly falling apart either due to a too-hasty construction process or because of having been left unattended or unused. There were however both doctors and patients present during this visit, but the majority of them were only there temporarily. The doctors were part of a mobile health clinic that had been brought in by a donation program initiated by a Danish charity foundation. The mobile clinic came once a year and provided free medical check-ups for the local population, undertaken by specialists from different medical fields of expertise. The reason for this yearly donation was twofold. For one, many families in the region could not afford even basic healthcare, let alone the trip to Tbilisi in case special consultancy or treatment was needed. This formed the basis of the second purpose: providing the specialized consultancy that was initially to have been performed at the hospital through tele-medicine.

There had, as Saakashvili went around the country on a string of hospital openings, been rumours that most of the hospitals were left empty as soon as the president and his entourage went home. That is, before the official openings a group of people would come in and insert hospital equipment of various kinds, but as soon as the hospital had been opened and the journalists had gone home, all of this equipment was packed up and transported to the next building being inaugurated – a road show of content for empty hospitals. Although this was on the level of hear-say (at least as far as we could verify at the time) it did reveal the local distrust existing towards the "100 hospitals" program, and accusations emerged that the whole thing was simply an excuse for setting up performative events where the president and his ministers could promote themselves and their make-believe achievements.

But other concerns were raised against the "100 hospitals" program by local and international organizations observing the process. Transparency International, for instance, raised a series of issues found to be problematic. One was that the speed of the project at large potentially endangered the quality of what was being built. Another was that in order to out-bid each other, investors had proposed to purchase many more hospital beds than what was required. The initial problem, dating back to the mid-1990s, of a healthcare sector with excessive and unused infrastructure, thus seemed likely to be sneaking back in. More problematic was the fact that new facilities only had to function as hospitals for seven years, and as many of the bidders in the tenders had turned out to be real-estate developers the long-term sustainability of the program was highly unclear. Finally, in many places where hospitals had been built, prices for healthcare services were unregulated. Oftentimes the quality of treatment was relatively poor compared to the costs, which proved problematic for large parts of the population with some being forced to rely on forms of self-medication that potentially deteriorated their health condition rather than improving it.[4] In short, while the "100 hospitals" program was officially represented as a successful endeavour to bring modern state-of-the-art healthcare facilities and expertise to the remote regions, the public hear-say of hospitals actually being empty from the very beginning, along with empirical evidence that some only worked because external actors such as international charity organizations had taken over responsibilities, and the critical analyses of the logics and practices informing the implementation program and its potential long-term effects, provided a bleaker image of the prestigious project.

Political theatre

Whether the "100 hospitals" program was actually a successful reformation and modernization of the healthcare sector; a performance of success with no substance as rumour had it; or a long-term accident waiting to happen as some analysts predicted; none of these readings immediately explain to us why the whole thing was apparently so amusing to many locals. What informed the irony and laughter at play when Katrine talked to Marina and Pati about the opening of the new hospital in Gori?

To Marina, events like this, and similar ones daily reaching her through the evening news, were ironic because of their unrecognizable relationship to the reality she saw herself as being a part of. The contrast between the reality depicted by Saakashvili in his speech at the hospital opening and Marina's personal experience with healthcare services was no less striking than the contrast between the president's depictions of economic prosperity and her daily reality of struggling to make ends meet, which we described in Chapter 2. In 2011, Emma – Marina's mother and our long-time strict Georgian teacher – suffered a severe stroke and was thereafter confined to her bed until she died in July of the same year. When Katrine visited the family in this period, Marina would repeatedly air her frustration about how to afford to take proper care of her mother. She explained how she was lucky that her childhood friend, Nino, was a doctor and could help out by drawing on her network and connections to examine and care for Emma. Marina's only perceived access to a proper doctor was thus through a childhood friend – and not through neither public nor private channels of hospitalization. The latter two would require unaffordable payments (either official or in the form of "appreciation"), and in Marina's opinion one could hardly trust such doctors anyway. Lack of money and lack of trust in the system therefore left her to use her personal network for healthcare.

The president opening new hospitals in the regions and promising accessibility to healthcare for all Georgians regardless of their background therefore seemed like pure fiction to Marina. And so did the cheering and clapping for the presidential performance. On the other hand, for her all of this was hardly surprising. On another occasion as she was cooking dinner, she jokingly remarked that we should open a restaurant and invite Misha. "He'll come to the opening of anything." Her statement vividly implied that to the president, the spotlight and a cheering audience was the essence – not the authenticity or quality of a given event. The talent for public performance and forceful poetic speeches that had gained Saakashvili his affectionate nickname "crazy Misha" when he first came into power, had at this time become too much for a growing number of people. It was no longer just a culturally cherished and recognizable style wrapping reasonable and pragmatic attitudes and actions. It was all there was.

Ironically, the "100 hospitals" program and the array of grand openings of the new buildings made the government vulnerable to public comparisons with the previous political regimes that they had tried so hard to distance themselves from through continuous reforms and articulations of freedom and democratic values, as put forth in Saakashvili's opening speech above. In parallel to the televised events, stories similar to that of Pati's, about how she was told by her school director to go and take part in the opening of the hospital, flourished in discussions among people on the street and around coffee tables. Those were stories evoking memories and depictions of Soviet political oppression and pretence achievements, and they confirmed and reinforced the sense that developments and public events were not what they appeared to be. Hence, the funny thing to Pati was not the event in itself, but rather that Katrine had been surprised to see so many people cheering for "Misha" in Gori. Her surprise was an indication of naiveté, an indication that she had not yet become familiar enough with contemporary Georgian politics for her to able to decipher the "fakeness" or pretence of such an event. That she apparently thought that the practice of present-day politics was in any significant way different from how politics had previously been practiced. That is, as it had been practiced in Soviet times. Pati's laughter represented a cynical assertion that the number of people present at an event like the hospital opening in Gori was not in any way an expression of the number of supporters for the president. It was simply a part of what people both now and then had to do in order to satisfy the official expectations of a public employee: that you, at least in public, support the government that is employing you. In the end, who wants to risk losing one's job over something as silly and ordinary as this?

So, Marina and Pati's laughter played on irony and cynicism rather than joy. An irony and cynicism connected to their confident recognition that most public political events such as the opening of the hospital in Gori were anyway staged; that people were either paid to go or indirectly threatened to. Whereas Katrine approached an understanding of the event from the point of view that it reflected some kind of reality – that a large number of locals were actually enthusiastic about the opening of the hospital and the speech given by the president – Pati's laughter cynically suggested that this was not at all to be expected. Everyone knows that, she seemed to imply. Knowing to what extent people were actually pressured to attend such events is of course difficult, as is knowing what the actual consequences would be if one was told to go but refrained from doing so. But rumours were plentiful. Several friends and acquaintances would reveal matter-of-factly that they – being teachers, employed at a local hospital or at a state museum – of course had to vote for the government in office if they wanted to be sure that they could keep their jobs. Political allegiance of any kind could not take precedence over the need to secure one's livelihood.

Coda: Misrecognition and cynicism

Returning to the public ideas of the opacity of politics in the previous chapter, the metaphor of politics as theatrical performance point us in the direction of the sociologist Erving Goffman's concepts of "frontstage" (what is performed to the audience) and "backstage" (what is said among the actors when the audience cannot see or hear; that is, when the performance is not "on").[5] Theatrical performance is a front, or mask, of a reality behind the scenes. The perception that something secret and publicly inaccessible was going on behind the facades of Saakashvili's political rhetoric was widespread indeed. In the case of the hospital openings, however, the cynicism seemed to refer not just to the awareness that what was staged was a facade for something else, but rather to the awareness that the political theatre was all there was; that there actually was nothing else – only a facade and nothing behind it.

The cynical reasoning of Pati – and to some extent also of Marina – mirrors the type of binary thinking that Alexei Yurchak critiques in academic analyses of Soviet authoritative discourse. That people act in public "as if" they comply with the authorities while privately believing something different. This, he argues, diverts attention from the continuing production and re-interpretation of discourse and knowledge.[6] To illustrate this point he uses the example of participants in a Communist Party meeting raising their hands in favour of a new resolution. Rather than necessarily meaning that they agree with the literal meaning of the resolution, the raising of hands may be a pragmatic answer to the question: "Are you the kind of social actor who understands and acts according to the rules of the current ritual, with its connection to the larger system of power relations and previous contexts of this type?"[7] In this analysis of late socialism, Yurchak distinguishes between semantic and pragmatic models of language. In late socialism, he argues, there was a shift from the semantic model (the idea that literal meaning was embedded in the linguistic form) towards the pragmatic model, in which reproducing the form increasingly gained precedence over attention to the literal meaning expressed through the form.[8] Building on this insight Yurchak and Dominic Boyer show in their article "American Stiob" how late liberalism operates under very similar discursive and ideological conditions to those of late socialism. Namely conditions in which there is an increasing "hypernormalization" of discursive form and performance, while literal or actual meanings behind these discursive forms become increasingly void.[9]

In many ways, the opening of hospitals in Georgia reflects the same principle; that there is (in this case very literally) a void behind the performance – everyone in the audience knows that the void is there, that the new hospital is likely both to be and to remain empty, yet still everyone continues to act as if this is not so in a very pragmatic and cynical fashion. Moreover, Yurchak and Boyer's analysis shows us how the question of form over content runs through late-Soviet socialism and late-liberalism alike, providing an answer to how and why people such as Pati so easily recognize remnants or aspects of Soviet politics in the government of Saakashvili's otherwise very anti-Soviet liberalism. As we shall see in the following chapter, both of these aspects – the question of form over content and a related conflation of Soviet and neoliberal political practice – were to become even more prominent on the eve of Saakashvili's post-revolutionary politics.

Chapter 9

The Emerald City

Something very, very special will take place

We return now to the shores of Adjara. On a sunny day in late April 2012 a man is giving a speech in Batumi. The speaker is standing in front of a giant poster that features an image of a grand hotel, and he is standing next to President Saakashvili – for whom he has nothing but praise. "Well thank you very much Mr. President", he begins,

> It's an honour to be here, it will be something very special. I have to start by congratulating George and your entire team because I've gotten to know George very well over the last year and he JUST – DOESN'T – STOP. He wants to make it great and that's why with Michael Cohen and the entire staff we decided to go forward, and we're really looking forward to it, and it's becoming even greater than we thought. And John, architecturally you and your staff have been amazing. But we will all admit, George and John, that the most amazing of all is the job the President has done in Georgia, it's such an honour, and for the people that live in Georgia you probably maybe are taking for granted what is happening – I will tell you outside of this area everybody in the world, they speak of Georgia as a great miracle that is taking place, and it's led by the President. So I just want to congratulate you, you are doing an amazing job, you're a big man outside of this area, they're studying you; they're writing books on him. So it's my honour, and I look forward to coming back many, many times. We had a fantastic evening last night, there's so much life, there's so much activity and I will be here many, many times, this is going to be something that is very, very special and

again John and George and everybody, I congratulate you, but most especially Mr. President, congratulations.

The "George" mentioned in the speech is Giorgi Ramishvili, chairman of Silk Road Group – one of the largest private investment companies in Central Asia and the Caucasus, and responsible for facilitating a number of investments in infrastructure, real estate and telecommunications in Georgia since 2004. The "John" mentioned in the speech is the American architect John Fotiadis, who designed the hotel, the upcoming construction of which is the reason for the press conference taking place. Dressed in a glass facade, it is to be a 47-floor building including apartments, clubs, a spa and a business centre comprising 160,000 square metres. Later the construction will be further developed with a seaside village and yacht club linked with Batumi Port. The man giving the speech is the American businessman Donald Trump, after whom the hotel was to be named: *Trump Tower*. It is estimated that Trump will be investing over 100 million USD in the project, with him noting that "Batumi is becoming quite a place, it's the best location, the Monte Carlo of the region".[1] In a later interview on the Fox News program *Fox and Friends*, he elaborates by stating to the interviewers that "I was in the Republic of Georgia over the weekend [...] and you have to see a place that's booming, it's unbelievable, it was a Russian satellite for a period of time, broke away, it's – you know, leaders are going to that country to find out what they're doing". One of the interviewers asks: "What's the industry there?" Trump: "Its everything! But one of them is tourism and what they're doing, they're building a place, Batumi, it's going to be one of the greatest places of the world within the next four or five years, I see what they're doing." Another interviewer asks, "What are you going to be investing in?" Trump: "Well, I'm doing a big job there, I'm doing a big development there, and it's been amazing".

Saakashvili had apparently been reading Donald Trump's book *Trump Never Gives Up* a few years earlier and had flown to New York on several occasions to meet with him in order to convince him to invest in Georgia. The approach worked and in 2011 a deal was signed during an event in Manhattan for Trump to license his name to two towers in Georgia that were to be the tallest ever built in the country.[2] One of them was to be the Trump Tower in Batumi, and another to be a similar one in Tbilisi. In the abovementioned interview on *Fox and Friends* Trump seems to give the impression that Batumi was an entirely new city. Although this was a slight overstatement, the city had certainly changed its appearance. Between 2007 and 2011 alone 35 hotels were built, dozens of others were planned, and the rapid urbanization and modernization of the city had moved far beyond "merely" painting facades into an almost complete alteration of the city's skyline.[3] Yet, despite the massive amounts of construction and re-construction that had taken place in Batumi, it was nothing compared to Saakashvili's next political vision: Lazika – a new major city that was in fact to be built from scratch.

Lazika

The plans to build Lazika were unveiled by Saakashvili a few months prior to Donald Trump's visit to Batumi. It was done on December 4th 2011 during a speech given in Zugdidi, a city located further up the Black Sea coast, not far from the border to Abkhazia and around 100 kilometres from Abkhazia's main city Sukhumi. "We have decided to build a big city between Anaklia and Kulevi, and to call it Lazika", Saakashvili told journalists and residents of Zugdidi. "In ten years' time, there will be a minimum of half a million people living in the city. It will be Georgia's second biggest city after Tbilisi, the main trading and economic centre in western Georgia, and Georgia's principal center on the Black Sea."[4] Costs for this grand project were estimated to be between 600 and 900 million USD, out of which the government was to contribute with around 20 percent and the rest to be paid by foreign investment groups, with Donald Trump among those mentioned.

Saakashvili further proclaimed that "we are founding a large city which from the start will be a lot bigger than Sukhumi is today, and which creates a clear basis for Georgia to regain its remaining territory, because Georgia naturally cannot be conceived of without Abkhazia". With the planned location for the new city only a few kilometres from the Abkhaz border, there was thus a clear secondary goal for Lazika in terms of territorial integrity. At this point the successful "return" of Adjara to Georgia in 2004 had slowly faded in light of the fact that there had been no developments in terms of South Ossetia and Abkhazia being reintegrated – if anything the war in 2008 had proven this to be a close-to-impossible feat. The proposed name of the new city symbolically reflected this secondary goal of territorial integrity. On the one hand, it made reference to the Laz people, an ethnic group native to the Black Sea coast of Georgia and Turkey. The territory of the kingdom of Lazika (or Lazica) had at one point included both present-day Abkhazia along with western Georgia and present-day Batumi before becoming part of the Kingdom of Georgia in the 11th century. On the other hand the city's name coincided with a new tracked infantry combat vehicle that had concurrently been developed by the Ministry of Defence for the Georgian Armed Forces. The name of the city-to-be and its territorial location, then, signified equally a carrot and a stick – the grandeur of Lazika would illustrate to the Abkhazians what great opportunities they were facing if re-uniting with Georgia, but also, connote the potential of being forcefully re-united by military means.

The Special Economic Region

Not long after Saakashvili's speech in Zugdidi, it was revealed that rather than merely building the city of Lazika, the project was to entail the construction of an entire region: the Anaklia Special Economic Region, covering a land area of around 200 square kilometres, with a planning period running up until 2020. A video clip depicting the total plan, made by Silkroad Digital Technology Co, was released shortly after Saakashvili's original speech. Starting and ending with an image of the Georgian flag, the clip featured animated aerial views of the proposed city alongside real-life footage of nature scenery, accompanied by grandiose music increasing in volume, and a voice-over describing central aspects of the project, subtitled in both Chinese and English. The latter went as follows:

> Combining the regional advantages and the opportunities brought about by the global economic circumstances, the Georgian government is planning to develop Anaklia and making it a special economic region in Georgia, hereinafter referred to as SER... Various functional zones will be planned within the SER. A 50-metres-wide forest-isolated area will be formed as a green ecological banner parting the SER and the surroundings. The total building area and exhibition area is about 3 million square metres. Leisure and residential areas will be classified into four levels including Level A, Level B, Level C and Level D, connected with international standard golf courses and urban landscaping.

At this point in the video an overview of the area shows the outline of the individual levels, ranging from Level A consisting of small houses sitting side-by-side, to Level D consisting of large-scale mansions. The voice-over continues:

> A transportation hub and logistics areas consisting of seaports, airports and warehousing could guarantee the fast turnover of the cargos and goods. The commodity processing zone will be the manufacturing and processing base of the

region, while a large amusement park and the wildlife park combine leisure, tourism and amusement together. There will be ten 5-star hotels of international standards surrounded by the beautiful landscapes, providing first class service and representing the full identity of the guest in a romantic atmosphere.

The development goals and direction are to transform Georgia into a nation with the most liberal economic environment, the most active economic development and the most eco-environment friendly nation. Anaklia SER will develop tourism industries, commodity processing industries, logistics, storage and transportation industries, as well as provide modern business services and financial service. The ambition is to make Georgia the most affluent country within the Trans-Caucasian Region through the effort of setting up a system encouraging economic cooperation and therefore attracting foreign investment. The development of Anaklia SER will greatly boost the economy of Georgia and brings about great tactical significance in promoting the international economic status of Georgia, making Georgia the economic hub within the Caspian Sea region and the Black Sea region, as well as important Eurasian regional highlight.

So, by taking advantage of the "opportunities brought about by the global economic circumstances", and by ensuring "the most liberal economic environment", the creation of Lazika and the Special Economic Region would boost the Georgian economy and cement the country's status as an economic and cultural hub of the Caspian and Black Sea regions. The idea had come to Saakashvili only a few months earlier while researching the development of pop-up or instant cities in China – a country with a significantly different economy and a significantly different population growth, one might object, and where the building of such cities had not altogether proven fruitful.[5] Nevertheless, the vision had taken hold to an extent that it seemed almost realized before constructions had even begun.

Architecturally, glass was to feature prominently in the construction of Lazika, and this was no coincidence. Glass had for long been a favoured building material for the Saakashvili government, and a series of police stations, along with other official buildings, had been erected throughout the country since the revolution. It had been a way to symbolize the transparency being promoted – allegedly making such places more accountable to the public. With the criticism surrounding the painting of facades, as described in Chapter 4, glass was a way to make sure that interiors were visible. And so, with inspiration from Trump and China, the glass city was revealed.

The mirage

Yet despite its grandeur, and the high-quality video clips describing it, news of Lazika was generally not well received. The head of the Centre for Civic Projects, Giorgi Khukhashvili, remarked following Saakashvili's speech in Zugdidi that this was merely "propaganda and PR designed to instill new hopes in the population" by a government that was short of resources. "I think", he continued, "the future of this project could best be read in the eyes of the regional government officials in western Georgia who were present when the president made this very unexpected announcement. There was horror in their eyes."[6]

And critical questions towards the Lazika project were abundant, from opposition leaders, journalists, civil organizations and ordinary citizens alike. How would it at all be possible to raise a city on an empty field in just four years' time? Given that the Free Economic Zone established in the nearby port city Poti in 2008 had not lived up to its promised boom in business and employment, why would Lazika? Exactly who would make up the proposed 500,000 residents? Why not support the severely challenged industrial cities already existing in Georgia instead, such as Rustavi and Zestaponi? How could a city of this size even be built in an area that largely consisted of swampland? What would happen to current landowners in the region? How could it not violate the nature preservation convention of parts of the region that had been signed back in 1997? And exactly who were all the foreign investors?

Colloquially Lazika came to be nicknamed "the Emerald City", referring to the capital city in Frank Baum's novel *The Wonderful Wizard of Oz* which lay at the end of the yellow-brick road. The novel describes how people entering the Emerald City are forced to wear green-tinted glasses. They are told to do so in order to protect themselves from the brightness of the emerald buildings, although it is in fact the glasses themselves that makes the city appear as emerald green. In reality it is not. The city is thus a humbug or a hoax created by The Wizard: a mirage attempting to make real something that is not. As a local resident, Kakha Pachkua, poignantly put it when asked what Lazika was: "Lazika is only one word – Lazika. There is nothing else."[7] Not unlike the ironic and giggling reactions of Marina and Pati to the hospital openings, quite a number of our Georgian friends and interlocutors would quite simply shrug and laugh cunningly when we brought up the subject of Lazika. Like our own intuitive reactions when hearing about the new magnificent project, they seemed to find it equally absurd or even farcical, but also not very surprising, that the president had come up with such a plan. However, despite the hail of criticism faced, Saakashvili was determined. A week before the parliamentary elections in October 2012, Saakashvili inaugurated the first buildings of Lazika, including the Town Hall and the future administrative building of the port. At this point, a total of around 42.5 million USD had already been spent by the state on Lazika. Simultaneously, the president published a video on his YouTube channel featuring his wife and son, as well as a group of children on a beach, drawing their "city of the future" in the sand, followed by an image of Lazika's would-be skyline.[8]

In many ways, the vision of Lazika and the Special Economic Region was the ultimate peak of the kind of millennialism and casino economy we described in Chapter 6. That is, the idea of surplus without production, that something can be created from nothing.[9] The visions presented in Saakashvili's speeches, the promotion footage we described above, and even Trump's enthusiastic admiration and belief in Saakashvili's projects, built on a logic that if only the (decided plan of) exclusive buildings and surroundings, the "shell", was in place, then the substance (inhabitants, wealthy foreign tourists, expertise, booming industries and trade, international economic cooperation, foreign investment, etc.) would appear on their own – out of nothing.

In this sense, Saakashvili almost seemed as if he was magician, yet, instead of ever actually pulling a rabbit out of his hat, he continuously brought a bigger and bigger hat on stage to wow the audience. Only, at this point, most of the audience no longer expected the rabbit to ever appear. But despite the fact that many Georgians shrug their shoulders at Saakashvili's plans for a new city and region, the plans were not without consequences. A report from the Netherlands Institute for Multiparty Democracy noted how political visions such as that of Lazika came to negatively affect the upcoming elections in terms of structuring the content of political debate. Or, perhaps more specifically: the *lack* of political content in these debates. "The sheer number of new ideas put out by the government", the report read,

> and the rapid rate of legislative change, makes much of the opposition's policy work obsolete or irrelevant. Furthermore, the government's penchant for big, headline grabbing initiatives naturally leaves the opposition on the defensive, having to act reactively, rather than pro-actively, and failing to offer an alternative vision. A representative of the Republican Party commented that instead of talking about urban planning

> policy, the party was instead forced to discuss President Saakashvili's plan for the new city of Lazika that is to be built on the Black Sea coast, and that instead of talking about 11 concrete policies in terms of healthcare reform, the party instead had to respond to the much promoted '100 hospitals' programme.[10]

It was obvious that Lazika did not – and most likely even could not – exist. However, as with the fake invasion presented in Chapter 7, this did not mean that the would-be city did not generate its own realities, not least in terms of partaking in determining what was being discussed both among ordinary citizens and among politicians. At the same time, it was also quite clear to the vast majority of the public that this was merely a performance, a theatre not unlike that of the empty hospitals.

Coda: Phantasm and future anteriority

With 2012 being an election year in Georgia, the plans for Lazika were seen by many as a desperate attempt on the side of Saakashvili to restore faith in his vision for Georgia's future. The opposition, on their side, were very clear in their position towards Lazika – if they won the elections, the project would immediately be abandoned. As the day of the elections approached in autumn 2012 the visions of Saakashvili had begun to overtake each other, leaving one project unrealized in the wake of another being envisioned. However, Saakashvili's dedication to Lazika remained particularly strong – even as its realization became questionable. "That's my ground", he told reporters during a speech in Kutaisi, "and I want my ashes spread there when I'm gone".[11]

During a discussion with Nana, a local Tbilisi-based NGO worker, in 2012, she told Martin that she believed Georgia to be in a state of pre-traumatic stress. Nana had been working with internally displaced people from the Georgian-Russian conflict, and for a series of years attempted to manoeuvre within the multitude of reforms that Saakashvili's government had been initiating within the sphere of psychosocial aid (and elsewhere). The present, she said, was not problematic because of what had happened in the past, but because of what had happened in the future. As a consequence, the precarity of life consisted not only of post-traumatic stress – a problematic past repeating itself – but also of pre-traumatic stress: a future that rendered problems in the present irrelevant despite their presence.[12] In short, for her the politics of the government were based on that which would have happened in the future; they were premised on future anteriority. In this view, politics, reform processes and proposed building projects alike came to operate as something that had already happened, although they were not yet reality – they did not work *towards* the future but *back from* the future. Indeed, future anteriority may be defined as a negation or a refusal of the present moment,[13] an absenting of the present, despite the continuous presence of the present. Lazika represents the pinnacle of this situation in that it partook in paralyzing political discussions of the present situation in favour of debates of a would-be future. In this sense, Saakashvili's visions as of 2012 were apt illustrations of what Begoña Aretxaga, writing from a different context, termed the phantasmatic qualities of politics in which fiction and reality come to constitute a kernel.[14]

In early 2015 Transparency International expressed concern about a series of construction and investment projects in Batumi having been halted, noting among other things that the Ministry of Finance and Economy did not have any information about the construction of Trump Tower, which at this point was still to materialize. Effective control over the fulfilment of investment had continuously been overshadowed by a political quest to attract new foreign investment and projects.[15] Aside from signing a letter of intent with the multinational development company Silk Road Group (which had been responsible for the aforementioned promo clip of Lazika), and cutting a ribbon by the then-as-now empty lot where Trump Tower was to be built, nothing had happened with Donald Trump's adventure in Georgia.[16] Further up the coast, the Lazika Pier Sculpture, a construction by J. Mayer Architects, was one of the few projects to ever be finalized in Lazika. Standing at the end of a 100-metre-long pier, the steel sculpture was, in the words of the architect, meant to reflect his preoccupation with "the way the real and the virtual is coming together".[17] Albeit unintentionally, the sculpture's location in Georgia's "Emerald City" only seems to support this vision.

Chapter 10

The Dreamer

Visions on the move

"On the face of it", Stephen Sackur says to Mikheil Saakashvili on an episode of BBC's *HARDtalk* airing on July 14th 2015, "this is one of the most bizarre political appointments I can ever remember. You were a national president, now you are regional governor in somebody else's country. What on earth is going on?" Saakashvili responds:

> Not just another country, not just another region, not just another time. Actually this is a very challenging time and everything I over-stood or fought for or dreamt about or stood up for basically is at stake in Ukraine. And Ukraine's fate on the other hand is at stake in Odessa… so it's a very unusual situation, we live in unusual times, and we need to make some unusual steps.

Saakashvili was appointed head of an International Advisory Council on Reforms in Ukraine in February 2015, and was appointed Governor of Odessa in May 2015. He had, before this, turned down an offer to become First Vice Prime Minister of Ukraine because this would have entailed him having to renounce his Georgian citizenship – although he ended up giving it up not long after. In the BBC interview, he explains that the reason why the Ukrainian president Petro Poroshenko wanted to bring him in was very obvious. Poroshenko knew what had taken place in Georgia during Saakashvili's leadership, and he wanted the same to happen in Odessa – both because of the high levels of corruption in the city, and because of Russia's annexation of nearby Crimea in 2014. Saakashvili's ambition was to assist in building a new Ukraine; he wanted to strike down on corruption, he wanted to turn the economy around, he wanted to bring back tourists, and he wanted to preserve democracy against the antagonism of Putin's Russia. And he had not come alone. With him came a series of people from his previous administration in Georgia, who were now occupying very prominent positions and offices within the Ukrainian government. Saakashvili was to do everything all over again, only this time in another country. Stephen Sackur goes on to ask,

> I understand your point that Ukraine is an incredibly important theatre right now where one of the most significant moments in Europe's modern history is taking place... but I just want to talk about Georgia for a minute. The former Prime Minister of Georgia, Mr. Ivanishvili, who of course was an opponent of yours, he says 'I pity our Ukrainian friends because Mr. Saakashvili's counsel may prove disastrous, his appointment there is dangerous for Ukraine.'

Saakashvili promptly and sternly responds: "Who cares what this man says!"

The main reason for Saakashvili's being in Odessa, of course, was that he had lost power in Georgia. So let us return for a moment to the parliamentary elections in 2012 mentioned in the previous chapter, and to the man who defeated him.

The secret billionaire

Reclusive or secretive were words often use to describe the businessman Bidzina Ivanishvili. With a private fortune matching some of the richest people in the world, he had, until he entered politics, been one of Georgia's main philanthropists. As mentioned in Chapter 4, he had been the main force behind sponsoring the building of the Sameba Cathedral in central Tbilisi, but besides this he had also funded the building of schools in his home region, and sponsored the pensions of around 3000 artists, writers and scientists – costs altogether estimated to amount to over one billion USD.[1] Eccentric was another word often used about him. He had built a grand house for himself overlooking Tbilisi that was referred to as a James Bond-like mansion, and he had penguins, lemurs and a zebra in one of his summer residences.

His entry into Georgian politics was sudden, but his aim was simple and clear: he wanted to remove Saakashvili from power as he believed the president had turned into a dictator and that "Soviet-style" politics had once again returned to the Georgian government.[2] "Georgian Dream" was originally a public movement launched by Ivanishvili in late 2011. By the time of the 2012 parliamentary elections, it had become a six-party coalition comprising very diverse ideological orientations, ranging from radical nationalists to pro-Western liberals – all, however, committed to the primary goal of removing Saakashvili.

Ivanishvili had lived in Russia when the Soviet Union dissolved and, as a consequence of this, he had automatically been given Russian citizenship. In 2010 he obtained French citizenship, which he later renounced seeking instead Georgian citizenship in order to be able to run in the elections. This, however, was denied by the Georgian authorities, and the opposition promptly responded to this by stating that the denial was politically motivated – the government, they held, feared that Ivanishvili and the Georgian Dream coalition were a real challenge to their power, and were doing everything they could to prevent him from running.

Ivanishvili had earned his money in Russia during the 1990s in banking, real estate and pharmacy, and despite selling off many of his Russian assets he still owned parts of Gazprom. These relations to Russia soon became a focal point of critique from Saakashvili and his supporters, and caused even some of the government's harshest critics to fear the alternative enough to prefer the status quo. Yet, Ivanishvili maintained that he wanted to reinstate commercial and cultural relations to Russia, noting that this did not mean he did not want to continue to work towards Euro-Atlantic integration or to reinstall territorial integrity in Abkhazia and South Ossetia. Only that these would be lengthy and difficult tasks. In general, despite their obvious antagonism towards each other, many of the proposed policies of Saakashvili and Ivanishvili were actually surprisingly similar, not least their policy of Euro-Atlantic integration. And, indeed, during the elections period Transparency International accused both Saakashvili and Ivanishvili of putting forth simplistic programs.[3]

Dreams and critical voices

Saakashvili was finishing his second term and he would not be able to run again during presidential elections scheduled for 2013. This meant that a series of initiated projects would have to be finished in order for him to prove that he had in fact achieved what he wanted during his time as president, and that the people of Georgia could safely choose his successor from the United National Movement as their new president. But public opinion was split, and a number of his previous supporters had turned against him. This was obvious when Martin met with Beka in 2012 at their summer home in Kiketi.

Beka and his sons are in full swing bottling and labelling red wine on the back porch. At this point Beka's enthusiasm for Saakashvili has completely vanished. He consistently refers to the president as an "idiot" and complains about the short-sighted perspectives inherent to his projects, not least the reconstructions in central Tbilisi that are still ongoing at this time. "Even my children are smart enough to know that this will not be possible within the time-frame he imagines", he said. Beka has, from time to time, been asked to become director of this or that project, given that he is a successful architect and entrepreneur. But he has consistently come up with excuses to avoid it, saying for example that he has fallen ill and is unable to carry out the task. He tells of one of his friends who, after a long life of hard work, had saved up a significant amount of money. Saakashvili forced him to build a hotel in Kobuleti by the Black Sea coast at the cost of several million lari. Now, says Beka, the friend has no money and he owns a hotel that only has customers two months a year, but which still needs staff, heating and maintenance during the remaining ten months – it is an extreme expense. He also complains about "Misha" having bought a private jet at the cost of 200 million lari, spending another 100 million on redoing the insides.

Beka is convinced that the election will be decided not by the Georgian population but by the US – if they want Saakashvili to go he will go, if not, he'll stay. He is, however, relatively sure that the Americans do not want him to stay in power; "They also think he's an idiot now. One of his last projects", he continues, "will probably be to abolish the lari so that the next president won't have any money." He laughs and continues with an explanation of how he thinks the country has become too focused on Europe and the US. For instance, he thinks it's a problem that there are so many English and American films on TV with Georgian subtitles, because they are too fast for the elder generation to be able to read. "Why can't they just dub them as they used to? When I was a child we were forced to learn Russian, now my own children are forced to learn English… There should be a TV channel, like Nostalgia in Russia, where they show old news broadcasts for the elderly to watch."

Beka was far from being the only one airing critiques of the apparent fixation with Europe and America and the lack of attention to the needs and sentiments of the elder generations. From the onset of his presidency Saakashvili had worked determinedly towards bringing young "clean" candidates into the state administration and the public sector at large. Replacing former officials and public employees had of course been an obvious strategy to disconnect the new administration from the corrupt and network-based system, which was seen as a remnant of Soviet and post-Soviet political practices. In effect, a seemingly unquestionable value of youth – signifying equally a break with the past system and progressive energy – had accompanied the incessant focus on reforms and rapid transformation over the years.[4] Whereas this logic might not in itself have been misplaced, it did increasingly alienate the elder generations who found themselves to be excluded from their previous professional positions and felt their experiences, expertise and, ultimately, societal function to be neglected.[5] The situation was amply illustrated in a conversation Katrine had with Maghvala and Nana, two women in their fifties, in the summer of 2011. During a discussion of their respective work lives and current unemployment, Nana said: "No one thinks about people anymore. The pensioner, the educated man, the scientist, the professor, the writer..." Nodding in confirmation Maghvala elaborated: "People of the age of 40 or more are no longer needed for jobs. People get experience and practice after the age of 45, but nobody needs these people. Only young people are needed. In this way the country will never be developed."

The political promises of Ivanishvili tapped into these grievances among the old intelligentsia and the elderly generations in general. As mentioned above, he had already personally sponsored the pensions of a number of artists, writers and scientists, which seemed to signify respect for mature experience and expertise, and which made his campaigning promises of higher pensions and general restoration of status and opportunities for these groups credible to many. Still, despite growing public criticism Saakashvili had by no means lost all of his supporters, and, to a majority of the people we talked to, it still seemed most likely that he and the United National Movement would stay in power.

The prison scandal and the result

One year prior to the elections, it was more or less unthinkable that a strong opposition would be able to appear and that there would potentially be a peaceful and democratic transfer of power as a result of the 2012 election. The popular saying "In Georgia we elect presidents by revolution" did indeed reflect the large-scale political developments in the country since the declaration of independence from the Soviet Union.

As noted above, Ivanishvili campaigned by representing himself and his Georgian Dream Coalition as the antithesis of the United National Movement and Saakashvili. And it seemed to be working. The campaign leading to the elections was heated and extremely polarized. The run-up was close. The fierce pre-election environment was severely intensified less than two weeks prior to the election date when videos were released to the public on September 18th showing inmates being raped and beaten in prisons. People were shocked and rallied in the streets of Tbilisi and other cities. Those we talked to about the case would say that of course they had heard of mistreatment happening in prisons. Somehow they knew – as they had long known so many other affairs in the country to be different from how they were represented. But still, having it exposed like this was different. It demanded a reaction, rather than merely a shrug. According to the opposition this revealed what was really going on under the surface in Saakashvili's regime and exposed the true face of the government – unmasked. To a large number of people, the footage proved that it was time for change.

Saakashvili and his government, on their hand, were swift to condemn the acts and promise to bring those responsible to justice. The staff from the prison were immediately fired and the Minister of Corrections, Khatuna Kalmakhelidze, resigned. Still, as we have encountered numerous times in the previous chapters, notably with regards to the Imedi hoax, the release of the videotapes also sparked speculations and counter-accusations. Several government representatives insinuated that the videos were part of a plot to destabilize the country prior to the elections, and the Ministry of the Interior issued a statement saying that the abuse was a set-up. "An investigation revealed that several members of the jail's security department had been involved in a plan to carry out abusive activities and record them", and "evidence shows that payments were made to coordinate and stage these appalling activities", it said.[6]

No matter the background for the appearance of the videos, or the general prevalence of the kinds of abuses they featured, they did, it seems, contribute to tipping the polls towards a victory for Ivanishvili and his coalition. In the end Ivanishvili's Georgian Dream coalition received 54.97 percent of the votes, while Saakashvili's United National Movement received 40.34 percent. The Rose Revolution era was over. In the days prior to the elections there had been outspoken worries that the elections would be a fraud, that Saakashvili would cling on to power, or that the elections would eventually erupt into civic unrest.[7] In other words, comments from international observers and our Georgian friends and interlocutors alike were very similar in that any change of power in the country was believed to most likely happen through yet another revolution. Numerous people – the two of us included – were proven wrong as the day of the election came and went.

Democracy at last?

> A quite extraordinary event has occurred in a small corner of the former Soviet Union. For the first time a majority ruling party has been ousted from power, not by a death (natural or otherwise), not by revolution and not by coup: Georgia's three million-odd voters have actually done it at the ballot box.[8]

On October 2nd, the day after the elections, Saakashvili conceded his defeat in a televised address; a move that led many of his former critics to respectfully recognize that he had now finally demonstrated that Georgia had "democratically matured" under his leadership. Or, as one analyst put it in retrospect, Georgia "remains the country in the former Soviet Union with [...] the most potential to take steps forward. The irony is that Mikheil Saakashvili has had to lose power to prove it."[9] Saakashvili himself later noted how his voluntary resignation had historical significance – respecting election results and the limits of a term had not been common practice in either Georgia or many other post-Soviet states, so his acceptance of his fall from power could be seen as a clear sign that democracy had really set in during his presidency.[10]

Having admitted his ruling party's defeat in the parliamentary elections, Saakashvili remained in office until the presidential elections in October 2013 after which he was replaced by the Georgian Dream candidate, Giorgi Margvelashvili. Shortly after his last day as president of Georgia he went into a self-imposed "exile", and by 2014 he had taken up residence in Brooklyn, New York. While there, he was soon to fall prey to a political practice he himself had been accused of employing very often, namely being denounced and prosecuted by the new government in power. Saakashvili had publicly announced that he hoped for John McCain, who had shown his undivided support for Georgia in the conflict with Russia, to succeed George W. Bush in the 2008 US presidential elections; and although Barack Obama, the eventual winner, never distanced himself from either Saakashvili himself or Georgia, it was a different relationship that the now-former Georgian President had with the US. Moreover, his former alma mater, Columbia University, had allegedly been reluctant to offer him a position due to concerns about the indictments he possibly faced, and eventually he was denied a work visa by the US authorities.

"There is something immensely sad about reading this", an

acquaintance of ours said once, as we were discussing a *New York Times* article on Saakashvili.[11] "Seeing him like this, despite any rightful criticism of what he did and didn't do, standing there in his colourful shorts, slightly overweight, drinking with a straw from a coconut." And there was somehow a sense of sadness in the article, or at least in the imprint it left. A former president once looked upon by many in the Western world as a beacon of democracy was now reduced to walking aimlessly around in the streets of New York, offering a journalist to take a picture of him on his bike, reminiscing about the time when a sheikh from the United Arab Emirates gave Georgia 20,000 palm trees, and the next minute describing how he had recently been denied access to a local New York restaurant because no-one knew who he was.

There is no doubt that Mikheil Saakashvili had dreams to change his country for the better, dreams that had eventually not been completely fulfilled. There is also no doubt that Bidzina Ivanishvili had dreams of doing the very same. Hence, in the same way as Beka of course is not the only winemaker and not the only individual to perform traditional and cultural virtues when possible, and Marina is not the only mother struggling to get by and being suspicious towards political ideas and visions, so neither Ivanishvili nor Saakashvili on their own can be said to be "the dreamer". The dreamer is much more of a figurative position, someone who has dreams on behalf of others. Others who may follow and take on those dreams – but also withdraw if those dreams do not materialize.

Coda: Nothing

Saakashvili's eventual political appointment in Ukraine raised a number of questions. Were his staff and programs in Odessa actually paid for by the US, as had often been the case in Georgia? What about the criminal charges he was facing for abuse of power, such as during the demonstrations in 2007 when police had used teargas and water cannons on people protesting against the government with accusations of corruption? Or, the accusations of him using public funds on everything from Botox injections, to renting a yacht in Italy, to buying artwork? Had he renounced his Georgian citizenship in order to avoid imprisonment in Georgia, as the Ukrainian constitution forbids the extradition of Ukrainian citizens? Was being governor of Odessa merely a stepping stone towards bigger aspirations, namely once again becoming president only this time in Ukraine?

After his appointment as governor, Georgians could read their former president remarking about Odessa that "there is no other city on the Black Sea, which can compete with its potential, with this wonderful city" and not help but wonder whatever had happened to Batumi.[12] While absence and emptiness, and forms without substance, as shown in the preceding chapters, were in many instances defining aspects of the afterlives of the Rose Revolution, it was the absence of Saakashvili himself that came to define its end.[13]

Ivanishvili had from the very beginning of his political campaign stated that he had no aspirations towards becoming president or staying in power – he merely wanted to make sure Saakashvili was not. Hence, as Saakashvili was replaced as president in 2013 and left the country, Ivanishvili resigned from his post as prime minister, leaving the office to his long-term political ally Irakli Gharibashvili. In spite of his early promises of stepping down voluntarily, the Georgian population was still left to wonder why Ivanishvili chose not to stay in politics. His departure from politics still seemed strange. And, with neither Saakashvili nor Ivanishvili (officially) present in Georgian politics, it seemed that there were no dreamers left. Without the theatrical performances, poetic speeches and dream-like visions for the future, it suddenly seemed like nothing was happening. "We have a joke here now", said Nana, the NGO worker we have met earlier, "that if only the president would go on TV and tell us all what time it is – at least then he would have said *something*".

For all his shortcomings, the string of unachieved goals, the megalomaniac projects, and the accusations against him of corruption and misuse of public funds, some people, including ourselves, were actually beginning to miss "crazy Misha" – at least he had known how to put on a good show. And, perhaps, this peculiar nostalgia towards Saakashvili and his time in office was the final proof that the revolutionary period was undoubtedly over. On the face of it, it belonged to the past.

Conclusion

Home

In the spring of 2014 Katrine visits Martin who at this time is conducting fieldwork in Tbilisi on the subject of nothingness. As has become a custom whenever we come back, we go to visit Marina. She still lives in the same apartment, but although the apartment looks much the same as when we lived there with the family years back, much in the household has also changed. Masha is now a grown woman, still residing at home, but slowly beginning to live her own life. The main difference of course is that Emma is no longer here.

Outside on the streets something is also missing on this particular day, May 26th. Despite it being Independence Day there are no grand exhibits of military equipment, as had been customary in the time of Saakashvili. Instead of troops and vehicles moving along Rustaveli with firefighters in the sky, this Independence Day features ordinary citizens strolling back and forth between numerous vendors, small stages where children are singing and dancing, sports activities and various performances. There are still a few tanks on display, but the mood is decidedly different from previous years.

The streets themselves are also very different. Years of construction and reconstruction have made their mark. Pastel shades are everywhere along with new, grand buildings constructed in glass: the new presidential residency finalized by Saakashvili in 2009, the "bridge of peace", and a series of new skyscraper hotels. But the building frenzy that had marked Saakashvili's last months in power in 2012, when the sounds of drills, sledge hammers, cut off saws, and bobcats had dominated the atmosphere of the city centre, has died out.

In the underground passageway something, however, has returned: the flutist. We see him on a few occasions but he doesn't seem to recognize us. Vanya and Gia, who had originally introduced us to him, are not around anymore. Vanya went to Russia a long while ago to take care of an ailing family member. After spending a few years roaming around Europe doing random work either on a tourist visa or as an illegal immigrant, he returned to Russia once more where he got married. Gia also left, first to the UK to study, then to Canada where he settled down with his family. He and the family come to Tbilisi for holidays during this spring, and we spend a night roaming around some of our old regular places, although the majority of the bars we used to frequent have closed down by now. New underground bars and cafés have popped up here and there, and a new generation of youths are on "birzha", hanging out on the streets at night. Also present on the streets of the city centre are the beggars, Roma and street children, despite the ardent efforts that had at one point been taken to remove them.

After having spent some days together in Tbilisi we take the train towards the coast, passing Gori along the way. Here, the change of central and local government, and the resultant circumvention of many of the key symbolic projects of Saakashvili, had sparked hope among some locals that the removal of the Stalin Monument would be reconsidered. Supposedly it was, and rumour had it that it would be re-erected in front of the Stalin Museum. At this point in time, however, the statue is still nowhere in sight. Further along, in Ambrolauri, the hospital remains only partly in use, still only fully functional when outside donors bring in the staff needed.

Late in the afternoon we arrive at the coast. We've decided not to stay in Batumi itself, but have instead rented some rooms in a small hotel in Kvariati further along the coast towards Turkey. It's both much cheaper and much quainter. If Tbilisi visually has become different after years of (re)constructions, it is nothing compared to Batumi, the cityscape of which has changed completely. But despite this change of appearance some things seem to have returned to what they were during our first visit here back in 2004. Local authorities have tacitly begun to accept the shadow economy increasingly governing the real-estate market – wealthy Russians and Ukrainians who have sought to get their money out of Crimea, hotels changing owners overnight, prostitution along the road from Batumi to the Turkish border, uncontrolled gambling – paradoxically reminiscent of the 1990s and the image Saakashvili originally sought to destroy. Meanwhile, the story of the mermaid has come to live its own life on various social media. In one account, it had not been brought to Tbilisi for re-examination but instead been put back into the sea where it was later caught and eaten by Russian soldiers. The evil had devoured the evil. Emil, along with most of the other young men among whom Martin conducted fieldwork in 2008 and 2009, is no longer here. Most are now in Russia, some in Turkey or Ukraine. A few have spent some years in prison, and a few have tragically passed away having lived short but harsh lives.

Further up the coast the Emerald City remains a mirage, and the area of Lazika and the Special Economic Region is once again becoming more and more of a marshland, a ruin even before it was built.

We don't manage to see Beka during our joint time in Tbilisi, but he is also a very busy man at this point. After years of perfecting his craft he has now become an award-winning winemaker, using ancient Georgian techniques of winemaking, and selling increasing quantities of his wine abroad. In some ways, Beka's success is the success the revolution was once believed to amount to; a strong economy and eyes towards the West seamlessly blending with an upholding of local, cultural traditions.

Afterlives of a revolution

A significant event takes place during this spring of 2014. Or rather, it doesn't take place: a gay parade. As in many other post-Soviet countries, being openly gay in Georgia has long been a near-impossibility. Indeed, on one of our first visits, Nina, Beka's wife, was looking through our guidebook and came across a section on gay and lesbian travellers which made her burst out laughing. "This is so strange, there are no homosexuals in Georgia so why would they write such a thing?" she said. This was not as such a question of antagonism on her behalf but rather a question of surprise. However, there were certainly antagonisms against the potential existence of a gay community and widespread consensus on the fact that if this indeed did exist it was inherently un-Georgian. If anything it was a problematic import from the West; a modern influence having nothing to do with traditional values.

While it had rhetorically and symbolically been possible to fuse the duality of tradition and modernity into a single ideal in the early years after the revolution by linking the nation's glorious past to aspirations of being a modern, European country, it had oftentimes proved a difficult task in practice. Aspirations towards the EU, for instance, had entailed the taking of many measures in order to live up to accession requirements, one such being protection of minorities – religious, ethnic and sexual. As an example, discrimination against sexual orientation in the workplace was prohibited already in 2006 and in 2012 the local LGBT organization "Identoba" organized the first ever public march in support of LGBT equality in the country taking place on May 17th, the International Day Against Homophobia. The march, however, was forcefully discontinued by a religious counter-demonstration, and the police proved unable (or unwilling) to stop violence from breaking out. Identoba later filed a complaint against the government's handling of the situation to the European Court of Human Rights, and on May 17th 2013, the LGBT rally took place once again. Unfortunately, this time the outcome was even more disastrous. Prior to the rally

Ivanishvili had stated that the LGBT community "has the same rights as any other social group",[1] while Patriarch Ilia II had denounced homosexuality as "an anomaly and disease", calling for a complete ban on gay rights.[2] Led by priests, some holding up chairs as a form of weaponry, thousands of Georgian Orthodox Church members covered the streets of central Tbilisi on May 17th, and, being asked to by the priests, the police refrained from taking action as the participants of the anti-homophobia rally were violently attacked near Freedom Square.

The event was a shock to everyone, but a divisive one. While some were horrified by the prospect of having to accept something such as homosexuality in order to become part of the EU, others were horrified by seeing their fellow countrymen express such extreme verbal and physical antagonism against a minority group. Divisions became even more outspoken in 2014 as the parliament unanimously passed a bill entitled "Elimination of All Forms of Discrimination". The bill created outrage among Orthodox groups who, supported by the Church, organized an "anti-anti-discrimination" rally. That year, Identoba chose not to organize any rally out of fear for the participants' safety. The atmosphere in central Tbilisi on May 17th 2014 can only be described as hateful, a day when many local voices were forced into complete silence. If the idea of the woman as a single or primary provider had become slightly more accepted during the preceding decade, this form of family structure was seen as a complete abomination. The divisive question of "modernity" versus "tradition" was thus still very much present, and it was clear that there were still many groups of people who were seen as misfits within society.

During the spring of 2014 Martin also goes to visit Nana, head of the NGO where he had conducted fieldwork back in 2006, to catch up on each other's lives as well as on recent developments in the country. "Today it's as if everyone is walking around with their eyes closed", Nana says of the current political situation.

"Nobody really knows what the government wants. When Ivanishvili entered politics I was against him because of his relation to Russia. It might not have been a problem – that was just the way I saw it. But now nobody really knows who the president is."

Although, as mentioned, there has been a halt in government construction and reconstruction, the cityscape is still changing. Only now it is not politicians but private investors and businessmen who undertake building and demolition. And something extraordinary is taking place, Nana says. Grassroots movements and activism have begun to appear, particularly among the younger parts of the population who are actively fighting against developments they don't agree with, for instance by blocking hotel constructions in Vake Park. In previous years, protests and rallies were events that had mainly been organized by political opposition parties and, as shown in Chapter 6, often participants of such events had been paid to come. Now people were starting to do it on their own.

The conversation also inevitably reaches the question of Crimea. At this particular point in time it was still uncertain exactly what would happen there. "There are still many inhabitants in Crimea who feel a strong relationship to Russia", Nana says. "In that way Ukraine is very different from Georgia. I was in Odessa in November last year, and when we came to the airport it felt like we were transported 30 years back in time. We were interrogated by the police, everyone spoke Russian to us." She believes Abkhazia and South Ossetia to be a lost cause by now. Russian aircrafts enter Georgian territory now and then, and she thinks that after Crimea it is a question of time before they also claim the two autonomous republics.

A year later, in mid-June 2015, a hippo could be seen walking the streets of Tbilisi, having escaped the local zoo. A few years earlier Tbilisi City Hall, whom the zoo belonged to, had decided to relocate it from the city centre to the outskirts of the city, near

Tbilisi Sea. An international architecture firm had devised a plan for an entirely new complex, but construction and relocation was delayed. On June 14th, the Vere River flooded due to heavy rains and a landslide that occurred some 20 kilometres outside the city. Besides resulting in the tragic deaths of at least 20 people, the flood killed nearly half of the animals in the zoo and left many others, including hyenas, bears, wolves, a white tiger and the hippo, wandering around in the streets during the days that followed.

In some ways, the flood became the pinnacle of absurdity: professional hunters roaming the streets, flocks of men seen attempting to push along a hippo, authorities catching a wolf in a suburb which turned out to merely be a dog, and an escaped penguin swimming 60 kilometres along a river to the border of Azerbaijan. In the midst of mourning over the tragic loss of human and animal life there was an abundance of jokes and irony over the absurdity of the situation – this was a theatre even surpassing empty hospitals or a pop-up city in a swamp. But amidst all this, a question also quickly arose: who was to blame? Some accused Saakashvili's government, some accused the Soviet period, some accused the current government. Speculations of conspiracies of various kinds were still abundant.

Clothes without an emperor and the spiralling of revolutions

When considering events taking place in Georgia in the years 2014 to 2015, over a decade after the revolution took place, it is easy to see how remnants of the phenomena taking place in the immediate aftermath of the Rose Revolution still continued to linger in various ways. Throughout the codas that have followed each of the preceding ten portraits we have deployed a series of analytical optics in order to unfold how the political ideas and visions underpinning the revolution gradually took on new, often unintended, lives of their own. These have ranged from questions of self-representation, dispossession, displacement, overwriting and ambivalence to scepticism, conspiracy, cynicism, phantasm and nothingness. What do such notions tell us about the afterlives of a revolution? We suggest that the emergence of these interrelated phenomena and sentiments points to a post-revolutionary reality that may be best described not as a linear progression towards set goals, but rather as a form of spiralling – as mutually reinforcing loops, rather than successive stages.

Hannah Arendt held that the idea of revolution has been a founding paradigm for the modern organization of political time.[3] Revolution has become an image of a society euphorically leaping into the future at points in time when people have been in desperate need of change.[4] The problem, as we hope to have demonstrated throughout this book, is that society rarely lands where it thought it would. Indeed, as Artemy Magun has argued in relation to revolutions on a broader level:

> The history of revolutions is neither a recurrent reproduction of identical phenomena nor (as in the vulgar Marxist model) a gradual sequence of progressive 'stages'. It presents us with a series of emancipatory movements, each of which fails to reach its ultimate goal, each of which stumbles in the middle of its course, only to be resurrected and radicalized by a new historical wave which stumbles again and flows back with all its unrealized might.[5]

Socialist or Marxist revolutionaries were a significant part of the 20th century, from the revolution in Russia to the post-colonial revolutions taking place around the world decades later. David Scott has noted how the leadership of Ronald Reagan in the US and Margaret Thatcher in the UK saw the rise of a new form of liberalism – neoliberalism – and the eventual fall of the Soviet Union gave rise to a new horizon; a new utopia of liberal democracy. In many ways this entailed that an era of Marxist politics of anti-imperialism and socialism vanished, leaving such revolutionaries as "leftovers from a former future stranded in the present".[6]

Modern historical time, Scott continues,

> has been organized around a notion of discrete but continuous, modular change, in particular, modular change as a linear, diachronically stretched-out succession of cumulative instances, an endless chain of displacements of before and after. Such succession, moreover, is progressive: change is improvement.[7]

For Marx, it was exactly this kind of succession that was revolutionary – it was what would enable humanity to overcome capitalism.[8] Yet, as Scott goes on to point out, such historical changes:

> no longer line up so neatly, so efficiently, so seamlessly, so instrumentally – in a word, so teleologically [...] what we are left with are aftermaths in which the present seems stricken with immobility and pain and ruin; a certain experience of temporal afterness prevails in which the trace of futures past hangs like the remnant of a voile curtain over what feels uncannily like an endlessly extending present.[9]

The portraits of this book provide empirical evidence supporting two aspects found in the perspectives on revolution recounted above. One concerns the question of afterlives and lost futures. Jacques Derrida famously coined the term "hauntology" in his *Specters of Marx* in order to move away from the ontological focus on presence to that of non-presence, and to that which has no being in itself but marks a relation to what is no longer or not yet.[10] This of course resembles our focus on afterlives and the traces of that which is no longer, or that which will never be, but which continues somehow to remain present. In the context of the Rose Revolution this may for instance be the myriad buildings constructed during Saakashvili's time in power that in different ways were meant to symbolize particular visions of the future, such as a future without corruption epitomized in glass police stations. These may well, in current everyday encounters with a corrupt official, lead people to become nostalgic towards the Rose Revolution era in terms of longing for a time when something was attempted to be done against corruption. Or, conversely, they may lead people to think about how that particular political project failed to work and hope for a new, grander political project to emerge and take over.

In *After the Future,* Franco "Bifo" Berardi refers to such situations as a slow cancellation of the future, and describes a modernity where expectations of different kinds are shaped within frameworks of forever progressive development: "the Hegel-Marxist mythology of *Aufhebung* and founding of the new totality of Communism; the bourgeois mythology of linear development of welfare and democracy; the technocratic mythology of the all-encompassing power of scientific knowledge; and so on".[11] What this in many places has come to entail is that even in the wake of widespread disappointment with a grand-but-failed political project, many people continue to look for another project to raise their expectations once again. This helps to explain why someone such as the NGO worker Nana, who had been critical towards Saakashvili and Ivanishvili alike, felt ambivalent in 2014 when none of these political figures were around anymore and suddenly she didn't know what the government wanted or who her current president really was. With the preceding chapters in mind, this leads to the conclusion that even though linearity functions both on the level of politics and the level or expectation, it rarely functions on the level of practice and it is exactly this discrepancy that allows for its continued repetition.

Another, related, issue we want to take up in relation to our empirical cases and the question of revolution is that of form and content. In the modern era, revolution, succession and change as organizing principles of political time have been inherent to communism, capitalism and neoliberalism alike. Hence, while "Marxist revolution" may have been discarded in many parts of the world as a political foundation for change, such as in Georgia, the organizing principle or *form* has remained the same despite the difference in political *content*, or ideology. This is something we have seen illustrated in several of the preceding chapters. In some cases it has been very literal forms such as such as the tourist infrastructure or newly built hospitals that have been empty of contents, but it has just as much been on the level of political practice in terms of performances and debates, most notably in the final three chapters. Cornelius Castoriadis and Vladimir Tismaneanu have respectively referred to this question of form without content as social imaginaries and fantasies of salvation.[12] The common ground between their two perspectives is their conclusion that capitalist modernity and communist modernity cannot be considered complete oppositions when seen in this light. On the contrary, they both work primarily on the level of form. This helps to explain why something like the plans to build Lazika was seen both as an expression of neo-liberalism and neo-bolshevism – a shared form with different contents where it was the form and not the content taking precedence.

Slavoj Žižek's notion of the decaffeinated society is revealing in this context. In *Welcome to the Desert of the Real* he notes how the modern world has become obsessed with products deprived of their properties – coffee without caffeine, cream without fat, beer without alcohol – but also how such forms without content exist in a wider sense: "what about virtual sex as sex without sex, the Colin Powell doctrine of warfare with no casualties (on our side, of course) as warfare without warfare, the contemporary redefinition of politics as the art of expert administration, that is, politics without politics".[13] And the list can be expanded even further, to "post-structuralism without cruelty, or Marxism without revolution".[14]

In the preceding chapters we have seen several examples of this; reforms without implementation; facades without interiors; hospitals without doctors; and city plans without a city. And what is interesting to note is how these various forms without contents seemed to gradually grow in size, without necessarily ever really leading anywhere, or without leading to where they were supposed to. Rather than the revolution and the decade that followed being a line of successive stages of improvement, it was more a question of spiralling occurrences that did create some forms of change, but which never in a linear fashion led towards the intended goal. Indeed, revolution may perhaps be characterized as a circular movement, or a constant return,[15] albeit not a return to the exact vantage point. One reason for this happening in Georgia has to do with the ways in which political forms, and performances of them, constantly increased. The visions and promises of Saakashvili grew increasingly utopian, and as we hope to have demonstrated through our portraits and their mutual connections and associations, it became gradually clearer that many of these visions and promises were in fact unachievable. Political representations and performances were increasingly de-coupled from the realities they supposedly referred to – the forms increasingly left without meaningful content. In terms of the notion of spiralling, the rings in the spiral continued to grow ever wider, increasing the distance to the starting point, yet never reaching an end point. Sentiments and phenomena such as scepticism, conspiracy, irony and perceived absurdity grew along with them.

What the revolution and its aftermath did seem to lead to in Georgia, however, was what we might term a reverse "emperor without clothes"; namely a situation where the clothes were present, but there was no emperor inside. There were, and are, numerous afterlives, remnants and traces of the Rose Revolution in present-day Georgia, but the man who epitomized the revolution itself has gone. Considering the ideal modernist paradigm of the revolution described above, one might even question whether the Rose Revolution was a revolution at all. Perhaps it was simply a shift of political power. It might not have been a revolution any more than coffee without caffeine is still coffee. That does not, however, mean that it did not have an effect – not least in terms of how people came to relate to it. And although many of its effects were unintended, effects were most certainly still there.

Summing up, when we consider the history of linear political projects and their failures we may argue that although the question of linearity could be said to provide a false promise – a political goal very likely to be unachievable in practice – it is perhaps the continued existence of this very form, and the resulting ambivalences, breakdowns, disappointments and after-lives, that eventually create changes; such as grassroots movements emerging in the wake of the Rose Revolution coming to an end. The clearest example of this, however, might well be that the intention of Saakashvili was certainly not for his own fall from power to become the symbol of democracy-at-last. The intention and direction of how this was to have unfolded was very different, but the result was still there.

Coda: Spectres of Misha

So revolution may be seen as a question of spiralling, something that simultaneously recedes from and approaches the same point, something that moves away and then returns but without returning to exact sameness as changes have happened along the way. For us, Georgia as a country has also become a question of constant returns, going back again and again after that first random visit in the summer of 2004. And, although going back increasingly became a return to familiarity in the sense that our relation to the country was strengthened over the years, it was never a return to a country that was unchanged.

This is markedly so when comparing our first visit to more recent ones, which certainly prove that many significant things have happened or changed. And although many parts of this book, and many of the voices presented, may be read as decidedly critical towards Saakashvili and his revolutionary project, it should not be forgotten that there were indeed tangible and substantial goals that were achieved during his time as president: the provision of public goods such as electricity, water and gas has largely been restored; the country's infrastructure has been rebuilt and developed; public employees are paid wages; the fundamental changes in the police force have caused a remarkable reduction in petty corruption and crime; foreign investment and touristm have increased significantly; and, finally, Georgia had its first transfer of political power by vote since independence from the Soviet Union. Donald Trump was perhaps right in asserting that Saakashvili had achieved something extraordinary – even if the achievements did not always match the even more extraordinary representations and performances accompanying them. In the end, whether this extraordinariness was positive or negative is a matter of judgment and in the eyes of the beholder. In spite of their critical voices, to most of the figures we have met in this book it has most likely been both.

The ten portraits that we have presented throughout this book are of course not exhaustive in terms of what one might have come across in Georgia from 2004 to 2014. They have been chosen here because they, from our perspective, are positions that each in their way illustrate aspects that a revolutionary reality relates to – or is forced to relate to: cultural and traditional stereotypes, family patterns, patriots, dreamers, mythologies, outcasts, performances, utopias. This is how and why, as we argued in the introduction, the ten portraits generate each other's context. It is through the variations, themes and mutual associations these portraits have entailed that we hope to have led readers closer to the interior of the revolution as a situation, and depicted the outcomes, consequences and afterlives of the revolution not merely on an explicitly political level but just as much on the level of daily life.

At the time of writing new figures are emerging in Georgia: The Hippo, The Chair-Holding Priest, The Activist, The Migrant. Some may be understood through previous figures or afterlives, as we have sought to do here. Others may represent novel configurations that will be defining for the next decade in the country. What the role of Saakashvili himself will be in this future context is impossible to foretell – as we have both come to learn, predicting political developments in Georgia is next to impossible. One thing is for sure though: one of the biggest differences for us when coming back to Georgia now is that Mikheil Saakashvili is no longer there. However, even in his current absence, the spectre of Saakashvili certainly still plays a role, and there are still plenty of stories to be heard about "crazy Misha". There have been many speculations as to whether he at some point will return to the political scene in his home country. But even if he does not, one thing that does seem predictable is that the spectres of him, his revolution, and the figures, positions and practices it generated, will remain present for some time to come.

Endnotes

Introduction

1 See for instance Peter Nasmyth, *Georgia: In the Mountains of Poetry* (New York: Routledge, 2006), 301.

2 Ann Laura Stoler, "Imperial Debris: Reflections on Ruins and Ruination", *Cultural Anthropology* 23, no. 2 (2008).

3 Martin Demant Frederiksen, *Young Men, Time, and Boredom in the Republic of Georgia* (Philadelphia: Temple University Press, 2013).

4 For an example, see Mark Fisher, *Ghosts of My Life: Writings on Depression, Hauntology and Lost Futures* (Winchester, UK: Zero Books, 2014).

5 Cornelius Castoriadis, *The Imaginary Institution of Society* (USA: The MIT Press, 1998); Vladimir Tismaneanu, *Fantasies of Salvation: Democracy, Nationalism, and Myth in Post-Communist Europe* (New Jersey: Princeton University Press, 1998).

6 Milan Kundera, *The Book of Laughter and Forgetting* (USA.: Harper Collins Publishers Inc., 1996 [1978]), 227.

7 See for instance Katherine Verdery, *The Political Lives of Dead Bodies: Reburial and Postsocialist Change* (New York: Columbia University Press, 1999); Tismaneanu, *Fantasies of Salvation: Democracy, Nationalism, and Myth in Post-Communist Europe*; Maruska Svasek, ed., *Postsocialism: Politics and Emotions in Central and Eastern Europe* (New York: Berghahn Books, 2006); Zlatko Skrbis, "'The First Europeans' Fantasy of Slovenian Venetologists: Emotions and Nationalist Imaginings", in *Postsocialism: Politics and Emotions in Central and Eastern Europe*, ed. Maruska Svasek (New York: Berghahn Books, 2006); Serguei A Oushakine, *The Patriotism of Despair: Nation, War, and Loss in Russia* (Ithaca: Cornell University Press, 2009).

8 See Mikhail Yampolsky, "In the Shadow of Monuments: Notes on Iconoclasm and Time", in *Soviet Hieroglyphics: Visual Culture in Late Twentieth-Century Russia,* ed. Nancy Condee (Bloomington London: Indiana University Press, 1995).

9 See Verdery, *The Political Lives of Dead Bodies: Reburial and Postsocialist Change;* Bruce Grant, "New Moscow Monuments, or, States of Innocence", *American Ethnologist* 28, no. 2 (2001).

10 See Mélanie Van der Hoorn, *Indispensable Eyesores: An Anthropology of Undesired Buildings* (New York: Berghahn Books, 2009); Victor Buchli, "Astana: Materiality and the City", in *Urban Life in Post-Soviet Asia,* ed. Catherine Alexander, Victor Buchli and Caroline Humphrey (New York: UCL Press, 2007); Caroline Humphrey, "Ideology in Infrastructure: Architecture and Soviet Imagination", *JRAI* 11 (2005).

11 See Stoler, "Imperial Debris: Reflections on Ruins and Ruination"; Kevin Platt, "The Post-Soviet Is Over: On Reading the Ruins", *Republic of Letters* 1, no. 1 (2009); Karolina Szmagalska-Follis, "Repossession: Notes on Restoration and Redemption in Ukraine's Western Borderland", *Cultural Anthropology* 23, no. 2 (2008).

12 Elizabeth Cullen Dunn, "Postsocialist Spores: Disease, Bodies, and the State in the Republic of Georgia", *American Ethnologist* 35, no. 2 (2008), 254.

13 Frederiksen, *Young Men, Time, and Boredom in the Republic of Georgia.*

14 See Joma Nazpary, *Post-Soviet Chaos: Violence and Dispossession in Kazakhstan* (London: Pluto Press, 2002); Caroline Humphrey, *The Unmaking of Soviet Life: Everyday Economies after Socialism* (Ithaca: Cornell University Press, 2002); Gerald Creed, "(Consumer) Paradise Lost: Capitalist Dynamics and Disenchantment in Rural Bulgaria",

Anthropology of East Europe Review 20, no. 2 (2002); Tova Höjdestrand, *Needed by Nobody: Homelessness and Humanness in Post-Socialist Russia* (Ithaca & London: Cornell University Press, 2009).

15 See Svetlana Boym, *The Future of Nostalgia* (New York: Basic Books, 2001); Peter Fritzsche, "How Nostalgia Narrates Modernity", in *The Work of Memory: New Directions in the Study of German Society and Culture*, ed. Alon Confino and Peter Fritzsche (Urbana: University of Illinois Press, 2002); Maria Todorova and Zsuzsa Gille, *Post-Communist Nostalgia* (New York: Berghahn Books, 2010); Daphne Berdahl, *On the Social Life of Postsocialism: Memory, Consumption, Germany* (Bloomington: Indiana University Press, 2010); Katrine Bendtsen Gotfredsen, "Void Pasts and Marginal Presents: On Nostalgia and Obsolete Futures in the Republic of Georgia", *Slavic Review* 73, no. 2 (2014).

16 See David Kideckel, *Getting by in Postsocialist Romania: Labor, the Body, and Working-Class Culture* (Bloomington and Indianapolis: Indiana University Press, 2008); Morten A. Pedersen and Lars Højer, "Lost in Transition: Fuzzy Property and Leaky Selves in Ulaanbaatar", *Ethnos* 73, no. 1 (2008); Adriana Petryna, *Life Exposed: Biological Citizens after Chernobyl* (Princeton, NJ: Princeton University Press, 2002); Mathijs Pelkmans, *Defending the Border: Identity, Religion, and Modernity in the Republic of Georgia*, ed. Pelkmans (Ithaca, NY: Cornell University Press, 2006); Alena Ledeneva, *Russia's Economy of Favors: Blat, Networking and Informal Exchange* (New York: Cambridge University Press, 1998); Elizabeth Cullen Dunn, *Privatizing Poland: Baby Food, Big Business, and the Remaking of Labor* (Ithaca, NY: Cornell University Press, 2004).

17 See Maria Louw, "Dreaming up Futures: Dream Omens and Magic in Bishkek", *History and Anthropology* 21, no. 3 (2010); Anne Line Dalsgaard and Martin Demant Frederiksen, "Out

of Conclusion: On Recurrence and Open-Endedness in Life and Analysis", *Social Analysis* 57, no. 1 (2013); Morten A Pedersen, "A Day in a Cadillac: The Work of Hope in Urban Mongolia", *Social Analysis* 56, no. 2 (2012); Galina Lindquist, *Conjuring Hope: Healing and Magic in Contemporary Russia* (New York: Berghahn Books, 2005).

18 See George E. Marcus, "Introduction to the Volume: The Paranoid Style Now", in *Paranoia within Reason: A Casebook on Conspiracy as Explanation*, ed. George E. Marcus (Chicago: University of Chicago Press, 1999); Harry G West and Todd Sanders, eds., *Transparency and Conspiracy: Ethnographies of Suspicion in the New World Order* (Durham: Duke University Press, 2003); Mathijs Pelkmans and Rhys Machold, "Conspiracy Theories and Their Truth Trajectories", *Focaal: Journal of Global and Historical Anthropology* 59 (2011); Katrine Bendtsen Gotfredsen, "Invisible Connections: On Uncertainty and the (Re)Production of Opaque Politics in the Republic of Georgia", in *Ethnographies of Grey Zones in Eastern Europe: Borders, Relations and Invisibilities in Eastern Europe*, ed. Martin Demant Frederiksen and Ida Harboe Knudsen (London: Anthem Press, 2015); "Enemies of the People: Theorizing Dispossession and Mirroring Conspiracy in the Republic of Georgia", *Focaal: Journal of Global and Historical Anthropology* 74 (2016).

19 See Alexei Yurchak, *Everything Was Forever, Until It Was No More: The Last Soviet Generation* (Princeton, NJ: Princeton University Press, 2006); Alexei Yurchak, "Suspending the Political: Late Soviet Artistic Experiments on the Margins of the State", *Poetics Today* 29, no. 4 (2008); Dominic Boyer and Alexei Yurchak, "American Stiob: Or, What Late-Socialist Aesthetics of Parody Reveal About Contemporary Political Culture in the West", *Cultural Anthropology* 25, no. 2 (2010); Tismaneanu, *Fantasies of Salvation: Democracy, Nationalism, and Myth in Post-Communist Europe*; Katrine Bendtsen

Gotfredsen, *Evasive Politics: Paradoxes of History, Nation and Everyday Communication in the Republic of Georgia* (PhD dissertation, Department of Anthropology, University of Copenhagen, 2013).

20 Lars Højer, "Escalations: Spying and Totalitarianism in Western China and Beyond", in *A Comparative Ethnography of Alternative Spaces*, ed. Jens Dahl and Esther Fihl (New York: Palgrave Macmillan, 2013).

Chapter 1: The Winemaker

1 See Paul Devlin, "Powertrip: Electricity Is Hope" (2004).

2 For depictions of Tbilisi's history and multiculturalism in the city see for instance: Ronald Grigor Suny, "The Mother of Cities: Tbilisi/Tiflis in the Twilight Empire", in *City Culture and City Planning in Tbilisi: Where Europe Meets Asia*, ed. Kristof Van Assche, Joseph Salukvadze and Nick Shavishvili (Lewiston: Edwin Mellen Press, 2009); Martin Demant Frederiksen, "'A Gate, but Leading Where?': In Search of Actually Existing Cosmopolitanism in Post-Soviet Tbilisi", in *Post-Cosmopolitan Cities: Explorations of Urban Coexistence*, ed. Caroline Humphrey and Vera Skvirskaja (New York, NY: Berghahn, 2012).

3 Paul Manning, *Semiotics of Drink and Drinking* (London: Bloomsbury, 2012).

4 Gerald Mars and Yochanan Altman, "The Cultural Bases of Soviet Georgia 2nd Economy", *Soviet Studies* 35, no. 4 (1983).

5 Florian Mühlfried, *Postsowjetische Feiern: Das Georgische Bankett Im Wandel*, (Stuttgart: Ibidem-Verlag, 2006); Laura Joy Linderman, "The Gendered Feast: Experiencing a Georgian Supra", *Anthropology of East Europe Review* 29, no. 2 (2011).

6 Mary Ellen Chatwin, "Tamadoba. Drinking Social Cohesion at the Georgian Table", in *Drinking: Anthropological Approaches*, ed. I. De Garine and V. De Garine (New York: Berghahn Books, 2001); Kevin Tuite, "The Autocrat of the

Banquet Table: The Political and Social Significance of the Georgian *Supra*" (Paper presented at the 2005 Conference on Language, History and Cultural Identities in the Caucasus, Malmö University, 2010).

7 See also Martin Demant Frederiksen, "Good Hearts or Big Bellies: Dzmak'atcoba and Images of Masculinity in the Republic of Georgia", in *Young Men in Uncertain Times*, ed. Vered Amit and Noel Dyck (New York: Berghahn, 2012); Tuite, "The Autocrat of the Banquet Table: The Political and Social Significance of the Georgian *Supra*".

8 See for instance Nora Dudwick, "No Guests at Our Table: Social Fragmentation in Georgia", in *When Things Fall Apart: Qualitative Studies of Poverty in the Former Soviet Union*, ed. Nora Dudwick, Elizabeth Gomart and Alexandre Marc (Washington, DC: World Bank, 2003).

9 Ancient (as well as more contemporary) Georgian political and cultural history has been described in several books, including for instance: Ronald Grigor Suny, *The Making of the Georgian Nation*, 2nd ed. (Bloomington: Indiana University Press, 1994); Jonathan Aves, *Georgia: From Chaos to Stability?* (London: Royal Institute of International Affairs, 1996); Jonathan Wheatley, *Georgia from National Awakening to Rose Revolution: Delayed Transition in the Former Soviet Union* (Aldershot, Hampshire; Burlington, VT: Ashgate, 2005); Stephen Jones, *Georgia. A Political History since Independence* (London: I.B.Tauris, 2013).

Chapter 2: The Mother

1 For descriptions of national perceptions of motherhood in Georgia see for example: Margharita Lundkvist-Houndoumadi, "Treading on the Fine Line between Self-Sacrifice and Immorality: Narratives of Emigrated Georgian Women", *Transcience Journal* 1, no. 2 (2010); Salome Tsopurashvili, "The Traditional Image of the Georgian

Phallic Mother and Her Crisis in Contemporary Women's Fiction" (MA dissertation, Central European University, 2008); Ana Rekhviashvili, "Nationalism and Motherhood in Contemporary Georgia" (MA dissertation, Central European University, 2010).

2 Dudwick, "No Guests at Our Table: Social Fragmentation in Georgia".

3 Humphrey, *The Unmaking of Soviet Life: Everyday Economies after Socialism*, 21.

4 Frederiksen, *Young Men, Time, and Boredom in the Republic of Georgia*, 27.

Chapter 3: The Misfits

1 Erin Koch, "Displacement, Health and Humanitarianism in Post-Soviet Georgia" (NCEEER Working Paper, www.nceeer.org, 2012), 7.

2 See Constanza Curro, "Davabirzhaot! Conflicting Claims on Public Space in Tbilisi between Transparency and Opaqueness", *International Journal of Sociology and Social Policy* 35, no. 7/8 (2015).

3 Dudwick, "No Guests at Our Table: Social Fragmentation in Georgia", 218f.

4 World Vision Georgia, "Street Children and Child Labour in Tbilisi: Coming from the Street Project" (Tbilisi: World Vision Georgia, 2007).

5 Downloaded from www.statistics.ge, June 2007.

6 Martin Demant Frederiksen, "The Would-Be State: Reforms, Ngos, and Absent Presents in Postrevolutionary Georgia", *Slavic Review* 73, no. 2 (2014).

7 Koch, "Displacement, Health and Humanitarianism in Post-Soviet Georgia"; Paul Manning, "The Hotel/Refugee Camp Iveria: Symptom, Monster, Fetish, Home", in *City Culture and City Planning in Tbilisi: Where Europe and Asia Meet*, ed. Kristof Van Assche, Joseph Salukvadze and Nick Shavishvili

(Lewiston: Edwin Mellen Press, 2009).

8 Frederiksen, "The Would-Be State: Reforms, Ngos, and Absent Presents in Postrevolutionary Georgia".

9 See Höjdestrand, *Needed by Nobody: Homelessness and Humanness in Post-Socialist Russia*; Svetlana Stephenson, *Crossing the Line: Vagrancy, Homelessness, and Social Displacement in Russia* (Basingstoke, UK: Ashgate, 2006).

10 Koch, "Displacement, Health and Humanitarianism in Post-Soviet Georgia", 8; see also Elizabeth Cullen Dunn and Martin Demant Frederiksen, "Introduction: Ethnographies of Absence in Contemporary Georgia", *Slavic Review* 73, no. 2 (2014).

11 See Lili Di Puppo, "The Construction of Success in Anti-Corruption Activity in Georgia", *East European Politics and Societies* 30, no. 1 (2014).

Chapter 4: The Pastel Shade

1 Quoted from www.freerepublic.com.

2 Quoted from Peter Finn, "Georgia Anticipates Bush Visit" (Washington Post Foreign Service, May 6th 2005).

3 The territory that today constitutes the eastern part of Georgia.

4 Quoted in Gela Mtivlishvili, "Movement Is Dangerous in European Sighnaghi" (www.humanrigths.ge, March 3rd 2010).

5 See Simon Seebag Montefiore, *Potemkin: Catherine the Great's Imperial Partner* (New York: Vintage, 2005).

6 Mtivlishvili, "Movement Is Dangerous in European Sighnaghi".

7 George Nonidze, "Tbilisi: Tearing Down the Past" (www.opendemocracy.net, November 23rd 2010).

8 Frederiksen, "'A Gate, but Leading Where?': In Search of Actually Existing Cosmopolitanism in Post-Soviet Tbilisi".

9 Named after the Georgian national Lavrentiy Beria who was

chief of the Soviet security and secret police (NKVD) under Stalin, and later Deputy Premier.

10 See for instance: Catherine Alexander and Victor Buchli, "Introduction", in *Urban Life in Post-Soviet Asia*, ed. Catherine Alexander, Victor Buchli and Caroline Humphrey (New York: UCL Press, 2007); Grant, "New Moscow Monuments, or, States of Innocence"; Paul Manning, "Rose-Colored Glasses? Color Revolutions and Cartoon Chaos in Postsocialist Georgia", *Cultural Anthropology* 22, no. 2 (2007); Pelkmans, *Defending the Border: Identity, Religion, and Modernity in the Republic of Georgia*; Szmagalska-Follis, "Repossession – Notes on Restoration and Redemption in Ukraine's Western Borderland"; Yampolsky, "In the Shadow of Monuments: Notes on Iconoclasm and Time".

11 Oushakine, *The Patriotism of Despair: Nation, War, and Loss in Russia*, 15.

12 Martin Demant Frederiksen and Ida Harboe Knudsen, "Introduction: What Is a Grey Zone and Why Is Eastern Europe One?", in *Ethnographies of Grey Zones in Eastern Europe: Borders, Relations and Invisibilities in Eastern Europe*, ed. Martin Demant Frederiksen and Ida Harboe Knudsen (London: Anthem Press, 2015).

13 Krisztina Fehérváry, *Politics in Color and Concrete: Socialist Materialities and the Middle Class in Hungary* (Bloomington: Indiana University Press, 2013), 1.

14 Sophie Arie, "Regeneration Man" (*The Guardian*, October 22nd 2003).

Chapter 5: The Soldier

1 Civil Georgia, "Saakashvili Addresses Nation on Independence Day" (www.civil.ge, May 26th 2006).

2 "'Georgia Decided to Restore Constitutional Order in S.Ossetia': Mod Official" (www.civil.ge, August 8th 2008).

3 Interview given by Saakashvili to CNN, August 8th 2008.

4 Civil Georgia, "Merabishvili on Elections, Opposition, Russia, Ukraine" (www.civil.ge, April 7th 2010).

5 "Merabishvili Responds to His Controversial Interview" (www.civil.ge, April 9th 2010).

6 One could argue that this idea of offering an occupying force money to demolish an unwanted monument, in many ways, proves continuities between the Georgian authorities and "undemocratic" practices rather than the opposite.

7 Giorgi Lomsadze, "Stalin Statue Purged in Hometown Gori" (www.eurasianet.org, June 25th 2010).

8 BBC, "Stalin Statue Taken Down in His Georgian Hometown" (www.bbc.co.uk, June 25th 2010).

9 Georgia was not invaded during WWII but it is estimated that the republic contributed more than 550,000 people to the Red Army out of its population of approximately 3,550,000. The population fell by 307,000 during the war years (see Suny, *The Making of the Georgian Nation*, 284).

10 Thomas de Waal, et al., "The Stalin Puzzle: Deciphering Post-Soviet Public Opinion" (Carnegie Endowment for International Peace, 2013), 2.

11 See also Gotfredsen, "Void Pasts and Marginal Presents: On Nostalgia and Obsolete Futures in the Republic of Georgia".

12 Civil Georgia, "Military Parade Marks Independence Day" (www.civil.ge, May 26th 2010).

13 Gerald Creed, *Domesticating Revolution: From Socialist Reform to Ambivalent Transition in a Bulgarian Village* (Pennsylvania: Penn University Press, 1997).

Chapter 6: The Mermaid

1 Frederiksen, *Young Men, Time, and Boredom in the Republic of Georgia*, 35.

2 Maria Louw, "Et Land Har De Uhyrer, Det Fortjener: En Beretning Om En Kirgisisk Seriemorder", *Jordens Folk: Etnografisk Tidsskrift* 43, no. 2 (2008).

3 For a classical example see the study of magic in Moscow by Lindquist, *Conjuring Hope: Healing and Magic in Contemporary Russia*; and for a description of pyramid schemes in Romania, see Katherine Verdery, "Faith, Hope, and Caritas in the Land of the Pyramids: Romania, 1990 to 1994," *Comparative Studies in Society and History* 37, no. 4 (1995). See also Maria Louw, *Everyday Islam in Post-Soviet Central Asia* (London: Routledge, 2007); Smoki Musaraj, "Tales from Albarado: The Materiality of Pyramid Schemes in Postsocialist Albania", *Cultural Anthropology* 26, no. 1 (2011); Pedersen, "A Day in a Cadillac: The Work of Hope in Urban Mongolia".

4 As argued in Jean Comaroff and John Comaroff, "Millennial Capitalism: First Thoughts on a Second Coming", *Public Culture* 12, no. 2 (2000).

5 For a further description of this see Yasmine Mursharbash and Henning Presterudstuen, *Monster Anthropology in Australia and Beyond* (London: Palgrave Macmillan, 2014).

Chapter 7: The Hoax

1 The full 30-minute report is available at www.youtube.com /watch?v=MS_5wuuaXRw&nohtml5=False (last accessed April 4th 2016)

2 Civil Georgia, "Eu Monitors Warn against Fake Tv Report" (www.civil.ge, March 16th 2010).

3 Gotfredsen, "Enemies of the People: Theorizing Dispossession and Mirroring Conspiracy in the Republic of Georgia".

4 Civil Georgia, "Phone Tape Adds New Twist to Fake Tv Report" (www.civil.ge, March 16th 2010).

5 Ibid.

6 Pelkmans and Machold, "Conspiracy Theories and Their Truth Trajectories", 68.

Chapter 8: The Theatre

1 Mikheil Saakashvili, "The President of Georgia Addressed the Population of Gori, 11 January, 2012" (www.president.gov.ge [no longer available], 2012).

2 The following account is largely based on the report by Transparency International Georgia, "One Hundred New Hospitals for Georgia: How Long Will They Last" (www.transparency.ge, 2007).

3 Esther Fihl and Martin Demant Frederiksen, "Recommendations for Future Fair Trees Foundation Projects in Georgia" (University of Copenhagen, 2013).

4 Transparency International Georgia, "One Hundred New Hospitals for Georgia: How Long Will They Last".

5 Erving Goffman, *The Presentation of Self in Everyday Life* (Garden City, NY: Doubleday, 1959).

6 Yurchak, *Everything Was Forever, Until It Was No More: The Last Soviet Generation*, 16–18; see also Peter Sloterdijk, *Critique of Cynical Reason* (Minneapolis: University of Minnesota Press, 1987).

7 Alexei Yurchak, "Soviet Hegemony of Form: Everything Was Forever, until It Was No More", *Comparative Studies in Society and History* 45, no. 3 (2003), 486.

8 Ibid.

9 Boyer and Yurchak, "American Stiob: Or, What Late-Socialist Aesthetics of Parody Reveal About Contemporary Political Culture in the West".

Chapter 9: The Emerald City

1 Helena Bedwell, "Donald Trump May Invest $100 Million in Georgia Resort Tower" (www.bloomberg.com, April 23rd 2012).

2 Charles V. Bagli and Andrew E. Kramer, "Trump Signs Deal to Develop Two Towers in Georgia, the Former Soviet State" (www.nytimes.com, March 10th 2011).

3 Tamta Khalvashi, *Peripheral Affects: Shame, Publics and Performance on the Margins of the Republic of Georgia* (PhD dissertation, Department of Anthropology, University of Copenhagen, 2015).

4 Nino Kharadze, "Georgian Leader Unveils Grand City Plan" (www.blog.xiphiasconsulting.com, December 12th 2011).

5 For a series of examples, see Michael Ulfstjerne, *The Un-Real Estate: The Social Life of Temporary Wealth in China* (PhD dissertation, Department of Cross-Cultural and Regional Studies, University of Copenhagen, 2015).

6 Kharadze, "Georgian Leader Unveils Grand City Plan".

7 Ellen Barry, "On Black Sea Swamp, Big Plans for Instant City" (www.nytimes.com, April 21st 2012).

8 Clément Girardot, "The Rise and Fall of Lazika" (www.thetuqay.com, March 25th 2013).

9 Comaroff and Comaroff, "Millennial Capitalism: First Thoughts on a Second Coming".

10 William Dunbar and Mikheil Svanidze, "Policy Development in Georgian Political Parties and Ngos" (Netherlands Institute for Multiparty Democracy, 2012), 11.

11 DFWatch, "Georgian President Plans Details of His Own Cremation" (www.dfwatch.net, May 3rd 2012).

12 Frederiksen, "The Would-Be State: Reforms, Ngos, and Absent Presents in Postrevolutionary Georgia".

13 See for instance Lisa Walsh, "Between Maternity and Paternity: Figuring Ethical Subjectivity", *Differences: A Journal of Feminist Cultural Studies* 12, no. 1 (2001); Frederiksen, "The Would-Be State: Reforms, Ngos, and Absent Presents in Postrevolutionary Georgia".

14 Begoña Aretxaga, *States of Terror: Begoña Aretxaga's Essays* (Reno: University of Nevada Press, 2005); Frederiksen, "The Would-Be State: Reforms, Ngos, and Absent Presents in Postrevolutionary Georgia"; see also Yael Navaro-Yashin, "Introduction: Fantasy and the Real in the Work of Begoña

Aretxaga", *Anthropological Theory* 7, no. 1 (2007).

15 Transparency International Georgia, "Hotel Construction in Batumi" (www.tranparency.ge, February 17th 2015).

16 Giorgi Lomsadze, "Donald Trump: Thinking Big in Azerbaijan" (www.eurasianet.org, July 13th 2015).

17 Deane Madsen, "Pier Sculpture" (www.architecturemagazine.com, November 12th 2013).

Chapter 10: The Dreamer

1 Jamie Doward, "I'm Not a Spy or an Oligarch, Says Georgia's Secret Billionaire" (www.theguardian.com, December 3rd 2011).

2 Luke Harding, "Bidzina Ivanishvili: The Eccentric Billionaire Chasing Georgia's Leadership" (www.theguardian.com, October 1st 2012).

3 Ibid.

4 Wheatley, *Georgia from National Awakening to Rose Revolution: Delayed Transition in the Former Soviet Union*, 200; see also Jones, *Georgia: A Political History since Independence*.

5 For an elaboration of these points see Gotfredsen, "Void Pasts and Marginal Presents: On Nostalgia and Obsolete Futures in the Republic of Georgia"; Gotfredsen, "Enemies of the People: Theorizing Dispossession and Mirroring Conspiracy in the Republic of Georgia".

6 *The Independent*, "Prison Abuse Scandal Rocks Georgia Election" (www.independent.co.uk, September 20th 2012).

7 See for example Thomas de Waal, "A Crucial Election in Georgia" (http://carnegieendowment.org, September 11th 2012); Damien McGuinness, "Georgia Election: Scandal and Intrigue Split Voters" (www.bbc.co.uk, September 29th 2012); *The Economist Europe*, "Pain and Grief in Georgia: Modernisation Is One Thing, Democracy Another: Georgia Faces a Dangerously Polarised Election" (www.economist.com, September 29th 2012).

8 James Nixey, "Update: Georgia Post-Election Analysis" (www.chathamhouse.org October 2nd 2012).

9 Ibid.

10 David M. Herszenhorn, "Exiting President Reflects on Georgia" (www.nytimes.com, November 17th 2013).

11 Jason Horowitz, "Exile in Brooklyn, with and Eye on Georgia" (www.nytimes.com, September 19th 2014).

12 de Waal, "A Crucial Election in Georgia".

13 Dunn and Frederiksen, "Introduction: Ethnographies of Absence in Contemporary Georgia".

Conclusion

1 Radio Free Europe, "Georgian Prime Minister Says Sexual Minorities Have Equal Rights" (www.rferl.org, May 15th 2013).

2 "Georgian Orthodox Church Leader Calls for Gay-Rigths Rally Ban" (www.rferl.org, May 16th 2013).

3 Hannah Arendt, *On Revolution* (New York: Penguin Classics, 2006).

4 Scott David Scott, *Omens of Adversity: Tragedy, Time, Memory, Justice* (Durham: Duke University Press, 2014), 4.

5 Artemy Magun, *Negative Revolution: Modern Political Subject and Its Fate after the Cold War* (New York: Bloomsbury, 2013), 2.

6 Scott, *Omens of Adversity: Tragedy, Time, Memory, Justice*, 5.

7 Ibid., emphasis in original.

8 See Derek Sayer, *Capitalism and Modernity: An Excursus on Marx and Weber* (London: Routledge, 1991).

9 Scott, *Omens of Adversity: Tragedy, Time, Memory, Justice*, 6.

10 Fisher, *Ghosts of My Life: Writings on Depression, Hauntology and Lost Futures*, 18.

11 Franco Berardi, *After the Future* (Edinburgh: AK Press, 2011), 18; see also Fisher, *Ghosts of My Life: Writings on Depression, Hauntology and Lost Futures*.

12 Castoriadis, *The Imaginary Institution of Society*; Tismaneanu, *Fantasies of Salvation: Democracy, Nationalism, and Myth in Post-Communist Europe*.
13 Slavoj Žižek, *Welcome to the Desert of the Real* (London: Verso, 2002), 10.
14 Bülent Diken, *Nihilism* (London & New York: Routledge, 2009), 2.
15 Magun, *Negative Revolution: Modern Political Subject and Its Fate after the Cold War*, 9–10.

Bibliography

Alexander, Catherine, and Victor Buchli. "Introduction." In *Urban Life in Post-Soviet Asia*, edited by Catherine Alexander, Victor Buchli and Caroline Humphrey. New York: UCL Press, 2007.

Arendt, Hannah. *On Revolution*. New York: Penguin Classics, 2006.

Aretxaga, Begoña. *States of Terror: Begoña Aretxaga's Essays*. Reno: University of Nevada Press, 2005.

Arie, Sophie. "Regeneration Man." *The Guardian*, October 22nd 2003.

Aves, Jonathan. *Georgia: From Chaos to Stability?* London: Royal Institute of International Affairs, 1996.

Bagli, Charles V., and Andrew E. Kramer. "Trump Signs Deal to Develop Two Towers in Georgia, the Former Soviet State." www.nytimes.com, March 10th 2011.

Barry, Ellen. "On Black Sea Swamp, Big Plans for Instant City." www.nytimes.com, April 21st 2012.

BBC. "Stalin Statue Taken Down in His Georgian Hometown." www.bbc.co.uk, June 25th 2010.

Bedwell, Helena. "Donald Trump May Invest $100 Million in Georgia Resort Tower." www.bloomberg.com, April 23rd 2012.

Berardi, Franco. *After the Future*. Edinburgh: AK Press, 2011.

Berdahl, Daphne. *On the Social Life of Postsocialism: Memory, Consumption, Germany*. Bloomington: Indiana University Press, 2010.

Boyer, Dominic, and Alexei Yurchak. "American Stiob: Or, What Late-Socialist Aesthetics of Parody Reveal About Contemporary Political Culture in the West." *Cultural Anthropology* 25, no. 2 (2010): 179–221.

Boym, Svetlana. *The Future of Nostalgia*. New York: Basic Books, 2001.

Buchli, Victor. "Astana: Materiality and the City." In *Urban Life in Post-Soviet Asia*, edited by Catherine Alexander, Victor Buchli and Caroline Humphrey. New York: UCL Press, 2007.

Castoriadis, Cornelius. *The Imaginary Institution of Society*. USA: The MIT Press, 1998.

Chatwin, Mary Ellen. "Tamadoba. Drinking Social Cohesion at the Georgian Table." In *Drinking: Anthropological Approaches*, edited by I. De Garine and V. De Garine, 181–90. New York: Berghahn Books, 2001.

Civil Georgia. "Eu Monitors Warn against Fake Tv Report." www.civil.ge, March 16th 2010.

———. "'Georgia Decided to Restore Constitutional Order in S.Ossetia': Mod Official." www.civil.ge, August 8th 2008.

———. "Merabishvili on Elections, Opposition, Russia, Ukraine." www.civil.ge, April 7th 2010.

———. "Merabishvili Responds to His Controversial Interview." www.civil.ge, April 9th 2010.

———. "Military Parade Marks Independence Day." www.civil.ge, May 26th 2010.

———. "Phone Tape Adds New Twist to Fake Tv Report." www.civil.ge, March 16th 2010.

———. "Saakashvili Addresses Nation on Independence Day." www.civil.ge, May 26th 2006.

Comaroff, Jean, and John Comaroff. "Millennial Capitalism: First Thoughts on a Second Coming." *Public Culture* 12, no. 2 (2000): 291–343.

Creed, Gerald. "(Consumer) Paradise Lost: Capitalist Dynamics and Disenchantment in Rural Bulgaria." *Anthropology of East Europe Review* 20, no. 2 (2002): 119–25.

———. *Domesticating Revolution: From Socialist Reform to Ambivalent Transition in a Bulgarian Village*. Pennsylvania: Penn University Press, 1997.

Curro, Constanza. "Davabirzhaot! Conflicting Claims on Public Space in Tbilisi between Transparency and Opaqueness."

International Journal of Sociology and Social Policy 35, no. 7/8 (2015): 497–512.

Dalsgaard, Anne Line, and Martin Demant Frederiksen. "Out of Conclusion: On Recurrence and Open-Endedness in Life and Analysis." *Social Analysis* 57, no. 1 (2013): 50–63.

de Waal, Thomas. "A Crucial Election in Georgia." http://carnegieendowment.org, September 11th 2012.

de Waal, Thomas, Maria Lipman, Lev Gudkov and Lasha Bakradze. "The Stalin Puzzle: Deciphering Post-Soviet Public Opinion." Carnegie Endowment for International Peace, 2013.

Devlin, Paul. "Powertrip: Electricity Is Hope." 2004.

DFWatch. "Georgian President Plans Details of His Own Cremation." www.dfwatch.net, May 3rd 2012.

Di Puppo, Lili. "The Construction of Success in Anti-Corruption Activity in Georgia." *East European Politics and Societies* 30, no. 1 (2014): 105–22.

Diken, Bülent. *Nihilism*. London & New York: Routledge, 2009.

Doward, Jamie. "I'm Not a Spy or an Oligarch, Says Georgia's Secret Billionaire." www.theguardian.com, December 3rd 2011.

Dudwick, Nora. "No Guests at Our Table: Social Fragmentation in Georgia." In *When Things Fall Apart: Qualitative Studies of Poverty in the Former Soviet Union*, edited by Nora Dudwick, Elizabeth Gomart and Alexandre Marc. Washington, DC: World Bank, 2003.

Dunbar, William, and Mikheil Svanidze. "Policy Development in Georgian Political Parties and Ngos." Netherlands Institute for Multiparty Democracy, 2012.

Dunn, Elizabeth Cullen. "Postsocialist Spores: Disease, Bodies, and the State in the Republic of Georgia." *American Ethnologist* 35, no. 2 (May 2008): 243–58.

———. *Privatizing Poland: Baby Food, Big Business, and the Remaking of Labor*. Ithaca, NY: Cornell University Press, 2004.

Dunn, Elizabeth Cullen, and Martin Demant Frederiksen.

"Introduction: Ethnographies of Absence in Contemporary Georgia." *Slavic Review* 73, no. 2 (2014): 241–45.

Dunn, Elizabeth Cullen, and Katherine Verdery. "Dead Ends in the Critique of (Post)Socialist Anthropology: Reply to Thelen." *Critique of Anthropology* 31, no. 3 (2011): 251–55.

Fehérváry, Krisztina. *Politics in Color and Concrete: Socialist Materialities and the Middle Class in Hungary*. Bloomington: Indiana University Press, 2013.

Fihl, Esther, and Martin Demant Frederiksen. "Recommendations for Future Fair Trees Foundation Projects in Georgia." University of Copenhagen, 2013.

Finn, Peter. "Georgia Anticipates Bush Visit." Washington Post Foreign Service, May 6th 2005.

Fisher, Mark. *Ghosts of My Life: Writings on Depression, Hauntology and Lost Futures*. Winchester, UK: Zero Books, 2014.

Frederiksen, Martin Demant. "'A Gate, but Leading Where?': In Search of Actually Existing Cosmopolitanism in Post-Soviet Tbilisi." In *Post-Cosmopolitan Cities: Explorations of Urban Coexistence*, edited by Caroline Humphrey and Vera Skvirskaja. New York, NY: Berghahn, 2012.

———. "Good Hearts or Big Bellies: Dzmak'atcoba and Images of Masculinity in the Republic of Georgia." In *Young Men in Uncertain Times*, edited by Vered Amit and Noel Dyck. New York, NY: Berghahn, 2012.

———. "The Would-Be State: Reforms, Ngos, and Absent Presents in Postrevolutionary Georgia." *Slavic Review* 73, no. 2 (2014): 307–21.

———. *Young Men, Time, and Boredom in the Republic of Georgia*. Philadelphia: Temple University Press, 2013.

Frederiksen, Martin Demant, and Ida Harboe Knudsen. "Introduction: What Is a Grey Zone and Why Is Eastern Europe One?" In *Ethnographies of Grey Zones in Eastern Europe: Borders, Relations and Invisibilities in Eastern Europe*, edited by Martin Demant Frederiksen and Ida Harboe Knudsen.

London: Anthem Press, 2015.

Fritzsche, Peter. "How Nostalgia Narrates Modernity." In *The Work of Memory: New Directions in the Study of German Society and Culture*, edited by Alon Confino and Peter Fritzsche. Urbana: University of Illinois Press, 2002: 62–85

Girardot, Clément. "The Rise and Fall of Lazika." www.thetuqay.com, March 25th 2013.

Goffman, Erving. *The Presentation of Self in Everyday Life*. Garden City, NY: Doubleday, 1959.

Gotfredsen, Katrine Bendtsen. "Enemies of the People: Theorizing Dispossession and Mirroring Conspiracy in the Republic of Georgia." *Focaal: Journal of Global and Historical Anthropology* 74 (2016): 42–53.

———. *Evasive Politics: Paradoxes of History, Nation and Everyday Communication in the Republic of Georgia*. PhD dissertation, Department of Anthropology, University of Copenhagen, 2013.

———. "Invisible Connections: On Uncertainty and the (Re)Production of Opaque Politics in the Republic of Georgia." In *Ethnographies of Grey Zones in Eastern Europe: Borders, Relations and Invisibilities in Eastern Europe*, edited by Martin Demant Frederiksen and Ida Harboe Knudsen. London: Anthem Press, 2015.

———. "Void Pasts and Marginal Presents: On Nostalgia and Obsolete Futures in the Republic of Georgia." *Slavic Review* 73, no. 2 (2014): 246–64.

Grant, Bruce. "New Moscow Monuments, or, States of Innocence" [In English]. *American Ethnologist* 28, no. 2 (May 2001): 332–62.

Harding, Luke. "Bidzina Ivanishvili: The Eccentric Billionaire Chasing Georgia's Leadership." www.theguardian.com, October 1st 2012.

Herszenhorn, David M. "Exiting President Reflects on Georgia." www.nytimes.com, November 17th 2013.

Horowitz, Jason. "Exile in Brooklyn, with and Eye on Georgia." www.nytimes.com, September 19th 2014.

Humphrey, Caroline. "Ideology in Infrastructure: Architecture and Soviet Imagination." *JRAI* 11 (2005): 39–58.

———. *The Unmaking of Soviet Life: Everyday Economies after Socialism*. Culture and Society after Socialism. Ithaca: Cornell University Press, 2002.

Höjdestrand, Tova. *Needed by Nobody: Homelessness and Humanness in Post-Socialist Russia*. Ithaca & London: Cornell University Press, 2009.

Højer, Lars. "Escalations: Spying and Totalitarianism in Western China and Beyond." In *A Comparative Ethnography of Alternative Spaces*, edited by Jens Dahl and Esther Fihl. New York: Palgrave Macmillan, 2013.

Jones, Stephen. *Georgia. A Political History since Independence*. London: I.B.Tauris, 2013.

Khalvashi, Tamta. *Peripheral Affects: Shame, Publics and Performance on the Margins of the Republic of Georgia*. PhD dissertation, Department of Anthropology, University of Copenhagen, 2015.

Kharadze, Nino. "Georgian Leader Unveils Grand City Plan." www.blog.xiphiasconsulting.com, December 12th 2011.

Kideckel, David. *Getting by in Postsocialist Romania: Labor, the Body, and Working-Class Culture*. Bloomington and Indianapolis: Indiana University Press, 2008.

Koch, Erin. "Displacement, Health and Humanitarianism in Post-Soviet Georgia." NCEEER Working Paper, www.nceeer.org, 2012.

Kundera, Milan. *The Book of Laughter and Forgetting*. USA: Harper Collins Publishers Inc., 1996 [1978].

Ledeneva, Alena. *Russia's Economy of Favors: Blat, Networking and Informal Exchange*. New York: Cambridge University Press, 1998.

Linderman, Laura Joy. "The Gendered Feast: Experiencing a

Georgian Supra." *Anthropology of East Europe Review* 29, no. 2 (2011): 22–50.

Lindquist, Galina. *Conjuring Hope: Healing and Magic in Contemporary Russia*. New York: Berghahn Books, 2005.

Lomsadze, Giorgi. "Donald Trump: Thinking Big in Azerbaijan." www.eurasianet.org, July 13th 2015.

———. "Stalin Statue Purged in Hometown Gori." www.eurasianet.org, June 25th 2010.

Louw, Maria. "Dreaming up Futures: Dream Omens and Magic in Bishkek." *History and Anthropology* 21, no. 3 (2010): 277–92.

———. "Et Land Har De Uhyrer, Det Fortjener: En Beretning Om En Kirgisisk Seriemorder." *Jordens Folk: Etnografisk Tidsskrift* 43, no. 2 (2008): 40–47.

———. *Everyday Islam in Post-Soviet Central Asia*. London: Routledge, 2007.

Lundkvist-Houndoumadi, Margharita. "Treading on the Fine Line between Self-Sacrifice and Immorality: Narratives of Emigrated Georgian Women." *Transcience Journal* 1, no. 2 (2010): 50–70.

Madsen, Deane. "Pier Sculpture." www.architecturemagazine.com, November 12th 2013.

Magun, Artemy. *Negative Revolution: Modern Political Subject and Its Fate after the Cold War*. New York: Bloomsbury, 2013.

Manning, Paul. "The Hotel/Refugee Camp Iveria: Symptom, Monster, Fetish, Home." In *City Culture and City Planning in Tbilisi: Where Europe and Asia Meet*, edited by Kristof Van Assche, Joseph Salukvadze and Nick Shavishvili. Lewiston: Edwin Mellen Press, 2009: 375–412.

———. "Rose-Colored Glasses? Color Revolutions and Cartoon Chaos in Postsocialist Georgia." *Cultural Anthropology* 22, no. 2 (May 2007): 171–213.

———. *Semiotics of Drink and Drinking*. London: Bloomsbury, 2012.

Marcus, George E. "Introduction to the Volume: The Paranoid

Style Now." In *Paranoia within Reason: A Casebook on Conspiracy as Explanation*, edited by George E. Marcus. Chicago: University of Chicago Press, 1999.

Mars, Gerald, and Yochanan Altman. "The Cultural Bases of Soviet Georgia 2nd Economy." *Soviet Studies* 35, no. 4 (1983): 546–60.

McGuinness, Damien. "Georgia Election: Scandal and Intrigue Split Voters." www.bbc.co.uk, September 29th 2012.

Montefiore, Simon Seebag. *Potemkin: Catherine the Greats Imperial Partner*. New York: Vintage, 2005.

Mtivlishvili, Gela. "Movement Is Dangerous in European Sighnaghi." www.humanrigths.ge, March 3rd 2010.

Mursharbash, Yasmine, and Henning Presterudstuen. *Monster Anthropology in Australia and Beyond*. London: Palgrave Macmillan, 2014.

Musaraj, Smoki. "Tales from Albarado: The Materiality of Pyramid Schemes in Postsocialist Albania." *Cultural Anthropology* 26, no. 1 (2011): 84–110.

Mühlfried, Florian. *Postsowjetische Feiern: Das Georgische Bankett Im Wandel*. Stuttgart: Ibidem-Verlag, 2006.

Nasmyth, Peter. *Georgia: In the Mountains of Poetry*. New York: Routledge, 2006.

Navaro-Yashin, Yael. "Introduction: Fantasy and the Real in the Work of Begoña Aretxaga." *Anthropological Theory* 7, no. 1 (2007): 5–8.

Nazpary, Joma. *Post-Soviet Chaos: Violence and Dispossession in Kazakhstan*. London: Pluto Press, 2002.

Nixey, James. "Update: Georgia Post-Election Analysis." www.chathamhouse.org, October 2nd 2012.

Nonidze, George. "Tbilisi: Tearing Down the Past." www.opendemocracy.net, November 23rd 2010.

Oushakine, Serguei A. *The Patriotism of Despair: Nation, War, and Loss in Russia*. Ithaca: Cornell University Press, 2009.

Pedersen, Morten A. "A Day in a Cadillac: The Work of Hope in

Urban Mongolia." *Social Analysis* 56, no. 2 (2012): 136–51.

Pedersen, Morten A, and Lars Højer. "Lost in Transition: Fuzzy Property and Leaky Selves in Ulaanbaatar" [In English]. *Ethnos* 73, no. 1 (2008): 73–95.

Pelkmans, Mathijs. *Defending the Border: Identity, Religion, and Modernity in the Republic of Georgia*. Ithaca, NY: Cornell University Press, 2006.

Pelkmans, Mathijs, and Rhys Machold. "Conspiracy Theories and Their Truth Trajectories." *Focaal: Journal of Global and Historical Anthropology* 59 (2011): 66–80.

Petryna, Adriana. *Life Exposed: Biological Citizens after Chernobyl*. Princeton, NJ: Princeton University Press, 2002.

Platt, Kevin. "The Post-Soviet Is Over: On Reading the Ruins." *Republic of Letters* 1, no. 1 (2009).

Radio Free Europe. "Georgian Orthodox Church Leader Calls for Gay-Rigths Rally Ban." www.rferl.org, May 16th 2013.

———. "Georgian Prime Minister Says Sexual Minorities Have Equal Rights." www.rferl.org, May 15th 2013.

Rekhviashvili, Ana. "Nationalism and Motherhood in Contemporary Georgia." MA dissertation, Central European University, 2010.

Sayer, Derek. *Capitalism and Modernity: An Excursus on Marx and Weber*. London: Routledge, 1991.

Scott, David. *Omens of Adversity: Tragedy, Time Memory, Justice*. Durham: Duke University Press, 2014.

Skrbis, Zlatko. "'The First Europeans' Fantasy of Slovenian Venetologists: Emotions and Nationalist Imaginings." In *Postsocialism: Politics and Emotions in Central and Eastern Europe*, edited by Maruska Svasek. New York: Berghahn Books, 2006.

Sloterdijk, Peter. *Critique of Cynical Reason*. Minneapolis: University of Minnesota Press, 1987.

Stephenson, Svetlana. *Crossing the Line: Vagrancy, Homelessness, and Social Displacement in Russia*. Basingstoke, UK: Ashgate,

2006.

Stoler, Ann Laura. "Imperial Debris: Reflections on Ruins and Ruination" [In English]. *Cultural Anthropology* 23, no. 2 (May 2008): 191–219.

Suny, Ronald Grigor. *The Making of the Georgian Nation.* 2nd ed. Bloomington: Indiana University Press, 1994.

———. "The Mother of Cities: Tbilisi/Tiflis in the Twilight Empire." In *City Culture and City Planning in Tbilisi: Where Europe Meets Asia,* edited by Kristof Van Assche, Joseph Salukvadze and Nick Shavishvili. Lewiston: Edwin Mellen Press, 2009.

Svasek, Maruska, ed. *Postsocialism: Politics and Emotions in Central and Eastern Europe.* New York: Berghahn Books, 2006.

Szmagalska-Follis, Karolina. "Repossession: Notes on Restoration and Redemption in Ukraine's Western Borderland." *Cultural Anthropology* 23, no. 2 (2008): 329–60.

Saakashvili, Mikheil. "The President of Georgia Addressed the Population of Gori, 11 January, 2012." www.president.gov.ge (no longer available), 2012.

The Economist Europe. "Pain and Grief in Georgia: Modernisation Is One Thing, Democracy Another: Georgia Faces a Dangerously Polarised Election." www.economist.com, September 29th 2012.

The Independent. "Prison Abuse Scandal Rocks Georgia Election." www.independent.co.uk, September 20th 2012.

Thelen, Tatjana. "Shortage, Fuzze Property and Other Dead Ends in Anthropological Analysis of (Post)Socialism." *Critique of Anthropology* 31, no. 1 (2011): 43–61.

Tismaneanu, Vladimir. *Fantasies of Salvation: Democracy, Nationalism, and Myth in Post-Communist Europe.* New Jersey: Princeton University Press, 1998.

Todorova, Maria, and Zsuzsa Gille. *Post-Communist Nostalgia.* New York: Berghahn Books, 2010.

Transparency International Georgia. "Hotel Construction in

Batumi." www.tranparency.ge, February 17th 2015.

———. "One Hundred New Hospitals for Georgia: How Long Will They Last." www.transparency.ge, 2007.

Tsopurashvili, Salome. "The Traditional Image of the Georgian Phallic Mother and Her Crisis in Contemporary Women's Fiction." MA dissertation, Central European University, 2008.

Tuite, Kevin. "The Autocrat of the Banquet Table: The Political and Social Significance of the Georgian *Supra*." Paper presented at the 2005 Conference on Language, History and Cultural Identities in the Caucasus, Malmö University, 2010.

Ulfstjerne, Michael. *The Un-Real Estate: The Social Life of Temporary Wealth in China*. PhD dissertation, Department of Cross-Cultural and Regional Studies, University of Copenhagen, 2015.

Van Assche, Kristof, Joseph Salukvadze and Nick Shavishvili, eds. *City Culture and City Planning in Tbilisi: Where Europe Meets Asia*. Lewiston: Edwin Mellen Press, 2009.

Van der Hoorn, Mélanie. *Indispensable Eyesores: An Anthropology of Undesired Buildings*. New York: Berghahn Books, 2009.

Verdery, Katherine. "Faith, Hope, and Caritas in the Land of the Pyramids: Romania, 1990 to 1994." *Comparative Studies in Society and History* 37, no. 4 (1995): 625–69.

———. *The Political Lives of Dead Bodies: Reburial and Postsocialist Change*. New York: Columbia University Press, 1999.

Walsh, Lisa. "Between Maternity and Paternity: Figuring Ethical Subjectivity." *Differences: A Journal of Feminist Cultural Studies* 12, no. 1 (2001): 79–111.

West, Harry G., and Todd Sanders, eds. *Transparency and Conspiracy: Ethnographies of Suspicion in the New World Order*. Durham: Duke University Press, 2003.

Wheatley, Jonathan. *Georgia from National Awakening to Rose Revolution: Delayed Transition in the Former Soviet Union*. Aldershot, Hampshire; Burlington, VT: Ashgate, 2005.

World Vision Georgia. "Street Children and Child Labour in

Tbilisi: Coming from the Street Project." Tbilisi: World Vision Georgia, 2007.

Yampolsky, Mikhail. "In the Shadow of Monuments. Notes on Iconoclasm and Time." In *Soviet Hieroglyphics: Visual Culture in Late Twentieth-Century Russia*, edited by Nancy Condee. Bloomington London: Indiana University Press, 1995: 93–112.

Yurchak, Alexei. *Everything Was Forever, Until It Was No More: The Last Soviet Generation*. Princeton, NJ: Princeton University Press, 2006.

———. "Soviet Hegemony of Form: Everything Was Forever, Until It Was No More." *Comparative Studies in Society and History* 45, no. 3 (2003): 480–510.

———. "Suspending the Political: Late Soviet Artistic Experiments on the Margins of the State" [In English]. *Poetics Today* 29, no. 4 (2008): 713–33.

Žižek, Slavoj. *Welcome to the Desert of the Real*. London: Verso, 2002.

Rebel Rebel

Chris O'Leary

David Bowie: every single song. Everything you want to know, everything you didn't know.

Paperback: 978-1-78099-244-0 ebook: 978-1-78099-713-1

Cartographies of the Absolute

Alberto Toscano, Jeff Kinkle

An aesthetics of the economy for the twenty-first century.

Paperback: 978-1-78099-275-4 ebook: 978-1-78279-973-3

Malign Velocities

Accelerationism and Capitalism

Benjamin Noys

Long listed for the Bread and Roses Prize 2015, *Malign Velocities* argues against the need for speed, tracking acceleration as the symptom of the on-going crises of capitalism.

Paperback: 978-1-78279-300-7 ebook: 978-1-78279-299-4

Meat Market

Female flesh under Capitalism

Laurie Penny

A feminist dissection of women's bodies as the fleshy fulcrum of capitalist cannibalism, whereby women are both consumers and consumed.

Paperback: 978-1-84694-521-2 ebook: 978-1-84694-782-7

Poor but Sexy

Culture Clashes in Europe East and West

Agata Pyzik

How the East stayed East and the West stayed West.

Paperback: 978-1-78099-394-2 ebook: 978-1-78099-395-9

Romeo and Juliet in Palestine

Teaching Under Occupation

Tom Sperlinger

Life in the West Bank, the nature of pedagogy and the role of a university under occupation.

Paperback: 978-1-78279-637-4 ebook: 978-1-78279-636-7

Sweetening the Pill

or How we Got Hooked on Hormonal Birth Control

Holly Grigg-Spall

Has contraception liberated or oppressed women? *Sweetening the Pill* breaks the silence on the dark side of hormonal contraception.

Paperback: 978-1-78099-607-3 ebook: 978-1-78099-608-0

Why Are We The Good Guys?

Reclaiming your Mind from the Delusions of Propaganda

David Cromwell

A provocative challenge to the standard ideology that Western power is a benevolent force in the world.

Paperback: 978-1-78099-365-2 ebook: 978-1-78099-366-9

Readers of ebooks can buy or view any of these bestsellers by clicking on the live link in the title. Most titles are published in paperback and as an ebook. Paperbacks are available in traditional bookshops. Both print and ebook formats are available online.